rhythms

DOWNLOAD THE
FIRST15 APP, AVAILABLE
FOR IOS AND ANDROID.

@FIRST15

FIRST15.ORG

© 2022 FIRST 15

All rights reserved. All photography used by permission - stock.adobe.com.

ISBN 978-1-7357630-3-3

Editing: Shayla Raquel, shaylaraquel.com
Design: Amanda Barnhart, ambarnhart.com

rhythms

PRACTICING THE

UNFORCED RHYTHMS

of GRACE

table of contents

All of life is built on rhythms. We wake, eat, work, play, and sleep. We listen and we respond. We hurt and we heal.

Whether it's the New Year or a random moment of spontaneity, sometimes I feel the urge to make a bunch of changes to my life. I want to sleep more and worry less. I want to do more but experience each moment fully. I want to connect with my friends and family, but I also desperately need meaningful time to myself.

Jesus makes an invitation in Matthew 11 that you and I need to hear as we begin a new year. Read this invitation slowly, fully taking in the meaning of each word:

> *"Are you tired? Worn out? Burned out on religion? Come to me. Get away with me and you'll recover your life. I'll show you how to take a real rest. Walk with me and work with me—watch how I do it.* **Learn the unforced rhythms of grace.** *I won't lay anything heavy or ill-fitting on you. Keep company with me and you'll learn to live freely and lightly."* (Matthew 11:28–30 MSG; emphasis added)

What we need is rhythms—good rhythms that, when practiced, lead us into a more vibrant, abundant life in every way that matters.

For the next four weeks, let's learn the "unforced rhythms of grace" together. Let's respond every morning to God's invitation to walk with him, to work with him, to watch how he does it. Let's center our time and energy on that which will make life better both for our sake and for the sake of those we love.

> *God, come and teach us the rhythms of grace,*
> *the rhythms of life that mold and fashion our days*
> *into a lifestyle of abundant living.*
>
> *Infuse every moment we set aside with*
> *your love, your voice, and your power.*
> *You are our teacher. We are your students.*
>
> *May new rhythms produce new life*
> *for your glory, and our good.*
>
> *Amen.*

connection

"Abide in me,

and I in you."

JOHN 15:4

Connection with the Divine

1

One of the quickest ways to change and growth is new rhythms—practices that weave moments together into wholly beautiful, life-giving days.

And when beginning new rhythms, there's no better place to start than looking at opportunities for meaningful connection. You and I were made to connect, to have authentic, façade-free relationships with God, ourselves, and others.

So today, we begin with a rhythm to connect with the divine, God himself in whom we "live, move, and have our being" (Acts 17:28).

SCRIPTURE

"Abide in me, and I in you." —John 15:4

Devotional

At the very start, before time and space began, was God. The divine wove himself into the very fabric of our universe. From subatomic particles to the whole cosmos, the Father, the Spirit, and the Son built existence and called it good.

And from the beginning of our Scriptures we see that in perfection, at the very beginning of our existence, God would walk with us as his people (Gen. 2). All was free from shame. All was free from death. All was free from toil.

Our connection with God was complete, pure.

With the introduction of sin into our humanity came brokenness in so many forms, but none worse than a broken connection with God. You and I were made first and foremost for pure, face-to-face connection with God. We were made to walk with God, to work with God.

And in the Old Testament we see one simple truth: when God's people centered their lives on connection with God, all was set right. But when God's people centered their lives on any other pursuit, whether it be wealth, status, beauty, or control, their communities would crumble.

But then came Jesus, our great restorer, the one who would set right what we made wrong. At his death the veil was torn in two, and now you and I are the very temple of God. God himself, the Holy Spirit, dwells in you and me.

And in Matthew 11, we find an invitation from Jesus an invitation to restoration of connection we must not miss today:

> *"Walk with me and work with me—watch how I do it. Learn the unforced rhythms of grace"* (Matthew 11:29 MSG).

As we look forward to setting new rhythms, what we need more than anything are rhythms that help us realize the full potential of our restored connection with God. In connection with God, we flourish. Outside of connection with God, our lives crumble.

Imagine if every day began with the singular pursuit of purely, wholeheartedly connecting with God. Imagine if your days were built on the foundation of knowing, not just mentally, but with your whole being, that God is good, real, present, powerful, and loving.

Our greatest enemy to living with pure, abiding connection with God is distraction. So, our greatest opportunity is the ruthless elimination of distraction.

If you will start your day by saying no to all the distractions that compete for your attention so you can say yes to God, the battle for your heart will be won.

If you will worship, read, and pray every morning, first thing, authentically connecting with your Creator, that connection will carry you through the inevitable ups and downs the rest of your day brings.

There are so many amazing rhythms that can help us connect with God. There is power in setting aside time at morning, noon, evening, and night. There is power in corporate worship, conferences, books, prayer meetings, and all the rest.

But if you are looking for one rhythm to carry you into all the other rhythms, start your day with the rhythm that matters most: a meaningful connection with the divine.

And practically, the piece of my morning rhythm that has helped more than any other piece in connecting with God has been making space to be silent, listen, and simply be with God.

May today's meditation serve as a powerful point of connection between you and a God who loves you more than words, music, or sentiment could describe.

MEDITATION

As we begin a time set aside for silence, making true space for God to fill, take a few moments to simply breathe. Breathe in deeply, and breathe out. And when you're ready, close your eyes, continue focusing on your breath, and simply rest in God's nearness.

CONVERSATION

Now, from a place of space and silence, begin a conversation with God. Allow these few points of conversation to serve as a guide:

1. Thank God, in your own words, for making a way for you to connect with him. Allow this verse to provide context for your thanksgiving:

   "And behold, the curtain of the temple was torn in two, from top to bottom." —Matthew 27:51

2. Ask God why he so desperately wants to connect with you, and take a few moments to listen to his response.

3. Ask God for one practical way you can better connect with him every day. Maybe it's making more space to be silent, or engaging in worship more, or beginning to connect with him more intentionally at noon or night. Wait for inspiration from the Holy Spirit, whom the Bible calls your *"Helper"* (John 14:26).

Conversation is one of the best ways we can connect with God, others, and even ourselves. I often find that God demonstrates his grace most with me in speaking so clearly, and filling me with so much encouragement, in even small windows of time.

ACTION

Set an alarm for a time today when you can reconnect with God and make space to reacknowledge the reality and goodness of God even just for a few moments.

Some great times to do that might be at 12:00, at 5:00 in the evening, or for five minutes before you intend to fall asleep. Also, in our First15 app, we have some great guided prayers for you to use to connect with God.

"He who keeps
understanding will
discover good."

PROVERBS 19:8

Connection with Yourself

2

One of the quickest ways to change and growth is by setting new rhythms, practices that weave moments together into wholly beautiful, life-giving days.

And when beginning new rhythms, there's no better place to start than by looking at opportunities for meaningful connection. You and I were made to connect, to have authentic, façade-free relationships with God, ourselves, and others.

So today, we focus on connection by inviting God to help us better connect with ourselves. May we grow in our understanding, love, and empathy toward ourselves. And may the fruit of a healthy connection be more understanding, love, and empathy for others.

SCRIPTURE

"Whoever gets sense loves his own soul; he who keeps understanding will discover good." —Proverbs 19:8

Devotional

When asked what the greatest commandment in all of Scripture was, Jesus answered with these words:

> *"You shall love the Lord your God with all your heart and with all your soul and with all your mind. This is the great and first commandment. And a second is like it: You shall love your neighbor as yourself."* (Matthew 22:37–39)

There are two vital, overarching points in these words we desperately need to grasp today. One, loving relationships are the singular point of life. Our life must be centered on loving God and loving others as ourselves. To pursue anything other than love is fleeting and futile.

Second, all three of these relationships are connected. The second commandment, Jesus says, is "like" the first. The way in which we love God impacts our relationship with ourselves and others. The way we love ourselves is directly correlated to our love for others. If we have thriving, loving relationships with God, ourselves, and others, then our life will thrive. But if any of these three are suffering, the others will suffer as well.

From my perspective, we have a strong focus as Christians for loving God and others. Many churches make these two commands their mission. While we may not in practice love God and others as well as we would hope, I don't believe that's for a lack of belief in importance.

But I fail to see near enough awareness or focus on our love for ourselves. Hardly ever do I hear sermons or read books where the emphasis is on teaching us to have a loving, thriving relationship with ourselves. In fact, that even sounds a bit heretical.

But ask yourself, just for a moment, how healthy are you emotionally? Do you have confidence in who you are, in who God has made you to be? Do you give yourself room to acknowledge when you are stressed, upset, anxious, lonely, or hurried?

How healthy are you mentally? Are there lies you're believing, thoughts about yourself that God himself would want to correct? Are you believing assumptions, things you think others believe about you that you couldn't be sure are true? If you could only choose whether you see yourself positively or negatively right now, which would you choose?

How healthy are you physically? Are you giving yourself the critical gift of rest? Are you allowing yourself the freedom to notice when your body is exhibiting signs of stress, anxiety, loneliness, or weariness?

If you were able to answer these questions, honestly believing that you were fairly healthy emotionally, mentally, and physically, how much more could you focus your loving attention on God and others? How much better equipped would you be to see others in need, and be able to minister out of the overflow of a truly abundant life? How much more could you authentically worship your Creator in all that you do, glorifying and bringing attention to him through your thoughts, words, and deeds?

Each day, you have an opportunity to connect with yourself in better, more life-giving ways. And how you do that boils down to one simple idea:

True self-love needs to be nothing more, and nothing less, than loving yourself as God does.

It is not selfish, or worldly, to love yourself the way God does. In fact, anything less than that is pride. To say that you should be different than how God made you, with your wiring, personality, and gifting, is to say that you know better than God does who you should be to accomplish his plans. To say that you should have had a different life is at minimum to discount God's ability to weave our stories together, even with all our brokenness, into a beautiful narrative that will ultimately be for his glory and our good.

So, with passion and fervor to focus on what might be the missing piece in Jesus's greatest commandments, how do we better lovingly connect with ourselves?

1. As you spend time alone with God every morning, take a moment to notice how you're doing. How are you feeling? What's weighing you down? What's bringing you excitement and joy? As you acknowledge those things, invite God into that place of self-awareness.

2. As you engage in worship, reading, and prayer, choose to love yourself as God does. Take ownership of his love. Believe in your self-worth, in your inherent value, and in the importance of your unique calling. And choose his perspective over your own, or what you believe the perspective of others to be.

3. As you go about your day, take just a moment to acknowledge your emotions and your thoughts, especially if they ever dip below the standard of an abundant life.

Acknowledge your stress, take a deep breath, and ask God for a pathway to peace. Acknowledge when you feel down on yourself, and thank God for his grace and ultimate plan. Acknowledge when you feel lonely, and courageously take the first step toward a relationship with others.

Like loving God and others, developing a vibrant and loving connection with yourself takes daily focus and attention. But also like loving God and others, that daily investment will produce more fruit than you can imagine.

Imagine a world filled with believers who are healthy, thriving, and empowered to love God and others well. Today, allow that dream to come to life in you, one thought, feeling, and action at a time.

Today's guide for meditation and conversation is a powerful opportunity to know and love yourself better. May God fill these next few moments with a tangible, life-transforming experience with his loving presence.

MEDITATION

As we begin a time of meditation, inviting God to increase our awareness, empathy, and love for ourselves, begin by taking a few deep breaths. Breathe in slowly, breathe out with intention. And receive a sense of God's presence with you, in and around you.

As you get to a place of calm, ask God simply for a sense of his love for you, and rest quietly, focusing on your breathing, in that sense of his love.

CONVERSATION

Now, from a place of sensing God's love, begin a conversation with your heavenly Father. Allow these few points of conversation to serve as a guide:

1. Reflect on the importance of loving yourself well. If you're hung up on that idea, journal why that might be. Be honest, and ask God for revelation and wisdom.

2. Where is the one place you need to love yourself better? Ask the Holy Spirit for revelation of his love for you in that area. Take time to join with his love.

3. What is one practical way that you can love yourself better today? What is one conversation you can have with a relationship that has been stressing you? What is one lie you can stop believing? What is one idea you can repeat to yourself when you feel down, or feel like you're failing?

Sometimes at the beginning of a better connection with yourself, life can feel a bit worse before it gets better. If we've avoided acknowledging ourselves for too long, there can be a bit of a mess. But like any other mess, it's just as real whether we acknowledge it or not. And the only true way forward is to see it and clean it.

I pray that First15 serves as a helpful guide to you in this process every morning. You can become healthy. You can learn to love yourself the way God does. You are unique, important, and valuable. May God "open the eyes of your heart" to see yourself as he does today (Ephesians 1:18).

ACTION

Find one person you are close with to open up about how you see yourself, the good and the bad. Ask them to simply listen, rather than correct as you begin. Take twenty minutes to bring into the light what has been hidden for too long. And if you feel safe, ask for and listen to the perspective of that person who loves you.

Until we see our perspectives and beliefs about ourselves for what they are, we'll never know just how much damage they're doing.

May today be a day of profound awareness, and even a bit of healing.

And may God bless you as you seek him.

"LET EACH OF YOU LOOK NOT ONLY TO HIS OWN INTERESTS,

BUT ALSO TO THE INTERESTS OF OTHERS."

PHILIPPIANS 2:4

Connection with Others

One of the quickest ways to change and growth is by setting new rhythms, practices that weave moments together into wholly beautiful, life-giving days.

And when beginning new rhythms, there's no better place to start than looking at opportunities for meaningful connection. You and I were made to connect, to have authentic, façade-free relationships with God, ourselves, and others.

So today, we focus on connection by looking at how we can, in health and with purpose, connect with others. May today stir our hearts to be known and to lovingly get to know others.

SCRIPTURE

"Let each of you look not only to his own interests, but also to the interests of others." —Philippians 2:4

Devotional

Maybe the hardest category of commandments in Scripture to take action on, at least for me, is loving others. Sometimes, a lot of times, people can just be the worst.

Honest to God (and I guess to you), I am often tempted to hole up somewhere, read and write forever, and let everyone else deal with loving actual people. It feels too easy, and too tempting at times, to simply connect with people online, on my terms, and avoid true, face-to-face connection with the messiness of people. And I don't think I'm alone.

With the now wholly pervasive rise of social media and smartphones, we could waste our entire life online, connecting with digital, curated versions of people and never meaningfully connect with others. We could be known only by our best moments, photos and videos taken in the best light, filtered and manipulated. And we could follow, read, and interact with only those who believe what we believe, make us feel good, and ultimately give us the experience at any given moment that we desire.

And that sounds really good, even almost perfect. Except we know that it isn't. We know that slowly, swipe after swipe, we are getting swept up into a system that isn't actually making our lives better.

When asked, people around the world said that technology both gives us the greatest opportunity for connection, but is also our leading cause of loneliness. Social media negatively impacts our stress levels, mood, anxiety levels, self-esteem, and conversations and has been proven to be highly addictive.

Scripture and our human experience are all too clear: life is about meaningful relationships. No amount of dollars truly makes us happy. (See the rise in depression and decrease in happiness in our world's richest 1 percent.) No amount of status, followers, recognition, or achieved goals gives us true, lasting peace or joy (just be honest with yourself). In reality, our lived experience is only as rich as our relationships with God, ourselves, and others. And rich relationship, while it can be enhanced with online connections, requires elements that cannot be replicated online.

God designed us, even physiologically, to thrive in meaningful connection with others. Did you know that when you hug someone, oxytocin is released into your body from the pituitary gland, lowering both your heart rate and cortisol levels (the hormone responsible for high blood pressure, stress, and heart disease)? Staring into the eyes of another human, whether a loved one or a stranger, has been proven to release oxytocin as well, the chemical responsible for the feeling of love and bonding.

But to experience the God-given goodness in connection with him and others, we're going to have to swim upstream in our current online culture. Take time today to reflect on the value of true connection and allow the Spirit to illuminate a path forward.

MEDITATION

Take a moment to quiet your heart and mind. Rest in the knowledge that you are wired for connection with God, with yourself, and with others.

CONVERSATION

Now, from a place of quiet in your heart and mind, begin a conversation with God:

1. Think for a moment about what it feels like to truly connect with others in a meaningful way. What happens in your body? How does it affect you?

"Two are better than one, because they have a good reward for their toil. For if they fall, one will lift up his fellow." —Ecclesiastes 4:9–10

2. What does it feel like when you're missing meaningful connection with others?

3. What is one practical way that you can foster meaningful connection with someone else today? Rather than waiting to be pursued, how can you pursue a meaningful relationship with another?

Realizing a gap in your life doesn't need to produce shame. The first step in moving forward is realizing the gap you want to close, and then trusting that God has you and will guide you. Shine a light on your life as clearly as you can and lean into any notion you have from the Spirit to where he is leading you.

My growth tracker   S M T W T F S

ACTION

Pursue a meaningful time of connection with someone around you today. Even just fifteen minutes spent away from screens and immersed in a meaningful relationship can change the nature of your day.

[1] The Economist, "Loneliness Is a Serious Public-Health Problem," September 1, 2018, https://www.economist.com/international/2018/09/01/loneliness-is-a-serious-public-health-problem.

"Your word is a lamp

to my feet..."

PSALM 119:105

Connection through Scripture

4

One of the quickest ways to change and growth is by setting new rhythms, practices that weave moments together into wholly beautiful, life-giving days.

And when beginning new rhythms, there's no better place to start than looking at opportunities for meaningful connection. You and I were made to connect, to have authentic, façade-free relationships with God, ourselves, and others.

And God has given us tools, incredibly meaningful ways that we can grow in our ability to foster a thriving connection with him, ourselves, and others.

So today, we focus on connection by looking at how Scripture provides a vital avenue to knowing and being known, to loving and being loved.

SCRIPTURE

"Your word is a lamp to my feet and a light to my path." —Psalm 119:105

Devotional

As high of a value as we place on Scripture as Christians, as strong of language as we use to describe the authority and merit of the Bible, something is fundamentally off about our approach to engaging with God's word.

The sentence I've written that has received by far the most negative feedback is:

"The Bible is not God."

Now, a portion of the negative feedback is warranted. There has been a severe mistranslation, or at least misteaching, in John 1 that is deeply confusing. John's gospel begins by saying, *"In the beginning was the Word, and the Word was with God, and the Word was God"* (John 1:1). So my statement that the Bible is not God seems in direct contradiction with John writing *"the Word was God."* That is, until you understand that John is actually talking about Jesus himself.

The Greek for *Word* is actually *Logos*, a term that would be better translated as "divine reason," or "the mind of God." But John 1:1 is maybe best clarified in simply reading through the next few lines. So, in context, John 1:1–4 says:

> In the beginning was the Word, and the Word was with God, and the Word was God. **He** was in the beginning with God. All things were made through **him**, and without **him** was not any thing made that was made. In **him** was life, and the life was the light of men. [emphasis added]

But beyond a misunderstanding of the true intent of John 1, I believe there is a deeper problem in our approach to God's word.

Growing up, spending time alone with God was a direct equivalent with reading the Bible. And still today, when I speak on the subject of spending time alone with God, I have people who come up to me to let me know that they read their Bibles every day.

The center of so many of our worship services is a teacher standing up, and across the better part of thirty minutes, unpacking the words of Scripture.

Here's why that's a problem: Scripture was never intended to be a substitute for God. The Bible was always meant to be an avenue to fully knowing its author, a way of connecting—heart, mind, and soul—with its Creator.

As humans, we tend to mold our life and experiences into that which we can control. We can control a time every day where we simply read and study a book. We can control a gathering once a week where educated teachers speak and apply principles from Scripture.

But what we need is not more things under our control. What we need is rhythms of giving God control. What we need is a Bible that guides us to its Author so that our time alone is centered on knowing and being known by God in an intimate, transformative, personal way. What we need is a service that invites God to show up in power, that courageously equips us to make space in our busy life for God to be the center, even when we don't know for sure where that will lead.

What we need is to reorient our engagement with Scripture as an avenue to connection instead of an end unto itself.

A. W. Tozer said it this way:

> If the Holy Spirit was withdrawn from the church today, 95 percent of what we do would go on and no one would know the difference. If the Holy Spirit had been withdrawn from the New Testament church, 95 percent of what they did would stop, and everybody would know the difference.

I believe the same sentiment applies to our time alone with God. And in that reality lies an immense opportunity.

You can connect with the God of the universe in an unexpected, personal, life-changing way every day. The Inspirer of the Bible himself wants to illuminate the pages of Scripture for you every day. And today, right now, as you make space to meditate and converse with the God of John, of David, the God who divinely ensured that you could have his word, anything and everything is possible.

Right now, decide to give God control over the next ten minutes and make space for him to simply be with you. May Scripture serve as a perfect guide to true, deep, meaningful connection with the God who loves you more than words could ever say.

 MEDITATION

As you take time to be still, fighting for even a few moments of quiet before the noise of the day, read these words from Psalm 46:10 slowly and carefully:

> *"Be still, and know that I am God.*
> *I will be exalted among the nations,*
> *I will be exalted in the earth!"*

Now lay those words before God and give up control today to the only one who actually has control. More than reading or understanding them, practice them right now.

Breathe in, and out, and be still in the presence of a personal, highly exalted God.

 CONVERSATION

Now, from a place of stillness, begin a conversation with the God of Scripture. Journal your thoughts and questions about God's word and invite him to give you wisdom and revelation today.

1. What questions do you have about Scripture, and how God wants to best use it in your life?

"This Book of the Law shall not depart from your mouth, but you shall meditate on it day and night, so that you may be careful to do according to all that is written in it. For then you will make your way prosperous, and then you will have good success." —Joshua 1:8

2. Where do you need wisdom and revelation today? Search for Scripture on the subject, or ask God to put an applicable passage on your heart and mind.

3. What verse do you need to be front and center today? Take time to pick a verse and ask God for revelation on it.

I've heard Scripture called a "manual for living," but the reality is that the Bible is so much more than that. A car manual, for instance, is a book written by a manufacturer or mechanic you'll likely never meet, and who cannot apply its pages and principles to your life.

But you have the Holy Spirit in you, and *with* you. The Author and Inspirer of Scripture longs to give you direct revelation on how to apply its value and principles to your circumstances.

Read, study, memorize, and engage with Scripture. But don't limit its power in your life by ending there. Allow God himself to use Scripture for higher, better purposes. And in doing so, discover what it's like to be a *"tree planted by streams of water that yields its fruit in its season, and its leaf does not wither"* (Psalm 1:3).

My growth tracker   S M T W T F S

ACTION

Pick one verse today and place it somewhere that you'll see throughout your day. Write it on your hand, make it your phone or computer background, write it on a sticky note at your desk. And allow it to foster and build meaningful, abiding connection with your heavenly Father who knows you and loves you.

"But I, through the
abundance of your
steadfast love, will enter
your house."

PSALM 5:7

Connection through Worship

5

One of the quickest ways to change and growth is by setting new rhythms, practices that weave moments together into wholly beautiful, life-giving days.

And when beginning new rhythms, there's no better place to start than looking at opportunities for meaningful connection. You and I were made to connect, to have authentic, façade-free relationships with God, ourselves, and others.

And God has given us tools, incredibly meaningful ways that we can grow in our ability to foster a thriving connection with him, ourselves, and others.

So today, we focus on connection by looking at how worship provides a meaningful pathway to connecting with God, ourselves, and others, not just physically or mentally, but with our full hearts.

SCRIPTURE

"But I, through the abundance of your steadfast love, will enter your house." —Psalm 5:7

Devotional

As I get older, and as my life gets more complicated, I struggle to make time for those more indirect pathways to meaningful connection with God.

Practices like conversing with God and reading Scripture feel like a more direct, measurable way to experience transformation and growth, whereas spending time worshipping, meditating, and being still seem harder to make time for.

But when I assess what's at the core of my struggle, I can see how desperately I actually need the unsure, the mystical, and the practices that mold and shape me even when I can't always explain how or why.

What I need most is worship.

The reality is that without worship, I am placing myself at the center of my own time alone with God. And I already suffer enough from placing myself at the center of my life and my story. What I need is for God to be at the center of my life and story. And that starts with taking something as simple as my first fifteen minutes of the day and centering my heart and mind on God.

And nothing re-centers me around the reality of God more quickly, or more authentically, than worship.

When I reflect on the lyrics of an anointed song and allow the music to wash through me, it almost miraculously connects me to God in a more holistic and transformative way.

Worship frees me to declare not just with my mind, but my heart, how good God truly is, and how worthy he is of my time, affections, and devotion. Worship somehow simultaneously shines a light to those places in me that aren't ready to express love and devotion to God, to parts of me that need healing and truth.

Every day, when you endeavor to read First15, especially if you're doing it in our app, there will be a temptation to push past the worship to those parts of your time alone with God that feel more direct and measurable, those elements that are easier and more in your control.

But don't miss the chance we give you every day to step outside of your control, to make space for God to do something deeper and richer than words can express or your mind can explain, to connect with your heart in spirit and truth.

Richard J. Foster, author of *Celebration of Discipline*, offers these thoughts on true worship. Allow them to convict and exhort you into an intentional choice to worship today:

> Worship is our response to the overtures of love from the heart of the Father. Its central reality is found "in spirit and truth." It is kindled within us only when the Spirit of God touches our human spirit. [2]

Worship, like all other disciplines, doesn't occur without investing in the practice with your whole heart. It's not about singing a melody or voicing lyrics. It's not about the time you set aside to stand and sing in a room of people. It's about his Spirit touching our spirit, his heart touching our heart.

So, as you move into a time of meditation and conversation, choose to take the next five minutes or so to bring who you are in this moment, the good and the bad, fully into connection with God.

Invite him in, rest in him, and discover the transformation that can only take place when his Spirit touches yours.

---

[2] Richard J. Foster, *Celebration of Discipline: The Path to Spiritual Growth* (New York: HarperCollins, 2018).

MEDITATION

As you begin to make space for God, set aside, even for a few moments, your desire to speak with or hear from God. Set aside the need to process or grow.

Take a few deep breaths, in and out, in and out, and invite God to fill the space you're making in and around you. And in the purest way possible, simply be with God. Rather than making this an exercise in personal growth, avail yourself to an intimate encounter with your Creator, and as you abide in his vine, the growth will come.

 CONVERSATION

Now, from a place of stillness, begin a conversation with the God who is so worthy of your worship. If you have a journal with you, process these guided conversation points with your journal:

1. What do you know, personally or authentically, to be good about God?

   "Ascribe to the LORD the glory due his name." — Psalm 29:2

2. What has God done in your life the times you've made space to truly worship him?

3. Ask the Spirit to illuminate in you those areas he wants to touch through worship. Journal or reflect on what keeps you from engaging in consistent, wholehearted worship. And talk with God about how you can practically spend more time centering your heart and mind on him in worship.

As you head out into the rest of your day, choose right now to engage with a worship song as you begin First15 every day. Practically, if you need to put some headphones by your bed, or choose to do First15 in a more private environment so you can engage with worship more fully, set a reminder to do that.

We even have playlists of worship for the weekday on most streaming platforms.

If a song selection isn't your preferred way to worship, use that element of First15 as a reminder to choose your own worship song to engage with.

Whatever you have to do, fighting to worship every day could be just the spiritual practice you need most to experience the fruit of a true, abiding connection with your loving heavenly Father.

ACTION

Choose one additional time today—maybe in the part of your day that could most use another meaningful moment of connection with God—and set a reminder to engage with one worship song.

In our First15 app, we have some great additional resources to help you spend more time in worship whether you're at work, at home, or on your commute. We have Spotify and YouTube playlists that are always updating with our favorite worship, and even some original worship songs to help you connect with God. Just search First15 Worship on your preferred platform to check it out.

"BE STILL AND KNOW

THAT I AM GOD."

PSALM 46:10

Connection through Meditation

DAY

6

One of the quickest ways to change and growth is by setting new rhythms, practices that weave moments together into wholly beautiful, life-giving days.

And when beginning new rhythms, there's no better place to start than looking at opportunities for meaningful connection. You and I were made to connect, to have authentic, façade-free relationships with God, ourselves, and others.

And God has given us tools, incredibly meaningful ways that we can grow in our ability to foster a thriving connection with him, ourselves, and others.

So today, we focus on connection by looking at how meditation empowers us to know God at a deeper level, in a place beyond image, words, or metaphor.

SCRIPTURE

"Be still, and know that I am God." —Psalm 46:10

Devotional

For me, the word *meditation* was a taboo concept.

When I started hearing about meditation, it was always in the context of Eastern religions, and in the category of spiritual practice that was deemed dangerous, and possibly demonic.

But a few years ago, I can honestly say that the well of my spiritual life had run dry. I was burnt out. I was exhausted. Worship, prayer, reading scripture and books—nothing that previously helped me connect with God was producing fruit.

And I was terrified.

I kept trying, and failing, to meet with God in a meaningful way. My relationship with him—and therefore my relationships with myself and others—had grown stale.

In that season, when I was struggling to know how to keep being the author of First15, and even at times how to feel comfortable in Christian circles,

I believe that God led me to the ancient Christian practice of meditation. As I sat, day after day, in silence, slowly but surely new water began to well up within me, and I found a deeper connection with God that infused my other spiritual practices with new life.

Psalm 1 begins this way:

> *Blessed is the man who walks not in the counsel of the wicked, nor stands in the way of sinners, nor sits in the seat of scoffers; but his delight is in the law of the* LORD, **and on his law he meditates day and night.** *He is like a tree planted by streams of water that yields its fruit in its season, and its leaf does not wither. In all that he does, he prospers* (Psalm 1:1–3; emphasis added).

It is not enough to read the Bible, or go to church, or talk about God with others. Those means cannot become our end. What we were created for is real, heartfelt, authentic connection with our Creator on the deepest level.

Scripture is most powerful not when we simply read it, but when we ruminate on its words and principles and allow the Holy Spirit to heal and transform us through it.

Church is most powerful when we don't just enjoy the company of our fellow believers and enjoy well-produced services, but when we allow God to make himself known in our midst, and to unify and empower us in a way only his powerful presence can.

And in our busyness, in our society that is so deeply distracted and inundated every moment of every day, what I truly believe we need most is silence.

It's in silence that we can learn to hear the still, small voice of God. It's in silence that we can allow God to do a work that is beyond measure, and beyond word or metaphor. It is in silence that we find the peace, rest, and love we were made for.

I honestly believe that it's from a place of inner quiet that the world will earnestly want what only God can give.

In Psalm 46:10, God speaks these words to you and to me:

> *"Be still, and know that I am God. I will be exalted among the nations, I will be exalted in the earth!"*

How often do you have true silence in your day? How much space is there where God has the chance to speak to you any and everything he would wish to?

In this daily devotional, we have created an opportunity every day to meditate on the goodness and nearness of God, to help guide you into a few moments of meaningful silence every day.

As you meditate today, and then have a conversation with God, try to stay quiet as long as you can. If your mind runs away, gently bring it back to a place of soft focus. And allow God to move in deeper, richer ways through the stillness.

May God do a profound work in your heart, mind, and body today as you make space for him to fill.

 MEDITATION

As you begin, take a few deep breaths, in and out, in and out, in and out. And slowly close your eyes and simply focus on your breathing.

In the quiet, release to God your anxieties and your hurry over to God.

And simply be still, for as long as you can.

 CONVERSATION

Now, from a place of stillness, begin a conversation with God. If you have a journal with you, process these guided conversation points with your journal:

1. What did you feel as you made space to be still?

   "Hear this, O Job; stop and consider the wondrous works of God."
   —Job 37:14

2. Ask God what he wants to do in your life through stillness and meditation. Write down or reflect on his response.

3. Now converse with God about those obstacles in the way of inner quiet. What is keeping you from being able to abide with God throughout your day?

In *The Weight of Glory,* C. S. Lewis wrote, "We live, in fact, in a world starved for solitude, silence, and private: and therefore starved for meditation and true friendship."

Meditation may be just the antidote you need for the busyness and noise of this world. If you're uncomfortable with the concept, wrestle with it a little longer. If you don't know how you'll find the time, look for twenty minutes in your schedule that you could cut. If you need some help, check out some of the resources below in our action section.

May God bless you richly as you seek him today.

ACTION

We are so used to the noise and busyness of life that spending meaningful time in silence every day can be almost unsettling.

As I was beginning my practice of meditation, I found a few resources to be deeply helpful.

One is a book called *The Cloud of Unknowing*, written by a Christian in the thirteenth century. And in our First15 app, there are several guided prayers to help you create a deeper connection with God.

But know that every day, in this devotional, you will be given a chance to be still and reflect on God in true quiet. I want to encourage you to deepen your practice every day, even by a few more moments, until you become comfortable in stillness.

May you find a deeper sense of inner quiet and peace today as you go about your day, and may God use that to draw others close to you and him. For his glory, and your good.

"Continue steadfastly

in prayer."

COLOSSIANS 4:2

Connection through Conversation

7

One of the quickest ways to change and growth is by setting new rhythms, practices that weave moments together into wholly beautiful, life-giving days.

And when beginning new rhythms, there's no better place to start than looking at opportunities for meaningful connection. You and I were made to connect, to have authentic, façade-free relationships with God, ourselves, and others.

And God has given us tools, incredibly meaningful ways that we can grow in our ability to foster a thriving connection with him, ourselves, and others.

So today, we focus on connection by looking at how conversation with God should and can be a cornerstone of our faith. May we grow in our desire to converse with our Creator, knowing conversation with him is indeed a two-way street.

SCRIPTURE

"Continue steadfastly in prayer, being watchful in it with thanksgiving." —Colossians 4:2

Devotional

Today, as we awaken to another twenty-four hours brimming with opportunity, there's an invitation from our Father waiting to be opened.

It's an invitation offered to us as God's children every day, whether we acknowledge it or not. And that invitation is to a time of true conversation with our loving Creator.

I've gone most of my Christian life unaware that God earnestly desires to talk with me. I heard stories from Scripture of moments God spoke to humanity, saw examples of those I deemed to have the privilege of conversing with God, but I never knew that I could have an honest conversation with my heavenly Father.

Then one day, out of sheer desperation, I asked God a question and actually desired a response. As I made even a few moments of space, with faith birthed out of need, I heard God speak.

I don't mean audibly, although I'll admit, I looked around to check. But I knew, beyond a shadow of a doubt, that God spoke clear direction to my heart in a way that could not be misunderstood. And that moment radically changed the trajectory of my life.

Colossians 4:2 is one of my favorite verses on the subject of prayer. Paul writes:

Continue steadfastly in prayer, being watchful in it with thanksgiving.

How often do you pray, and actually maintain a posture of watchfulness for God's answer? And how often do you maintain an attitude of thanksgiving in the midst of unanswered prayer?

For some reason, my default posture when I pray is still believing that God will indirectly say no to me. I wait for closed doors, or for another option to present itself. I struggle to maintain an attitude of thankfulness, believing that God can and will answer in a perfect way in the perfect time. And I struggle to believe that God is actually for me, that he wants truly good things for me.

The cornerstone of any thriving relationship is good communication. Communication means both individuals speak and listen well; they are *for* each other; and they make space to converse often enough to truly know one another.

And our relationship with God is no different.

God is inviting you and me to something so much more than a cosmic call-in line. He is inviting us, every day, into meaningful conversation with him. And that invitation is available to you right now.

May you talk with God in earnest and with thanksgiving and make space even now to be watchful for how he would answer.

May his voice raise the tide of your belief, drawing you deeper into an abiding connection with him.

 MEDITATION

Before conversing with God, take a few deep breaths, in and out, in and out, in and out. And slowly close your eyes and simply focus on your breathing.

Create space to set an expectation that you will not solely talk to God today, but you'll truly listen. Allow your desire to shift away from speaking to listening, believing that God already knows the desires of your heart and earnestly desires to speak to you today.

In the quiet, release your hurry to God. And from a place of peace with a posture of thanksgiving, follow this guide to conversation with your Creator.

 CONVERSATION

To help you gather your thoughts and write down what you sense God is saying, grab a journal if you can:

1. Ask God what he desires to speak to you today. And make space to listen.

   "God speaks in the silence of the heart. Listening is the beginning of prayer." —Mother Theresa

2. What's troubling you today? If you're unsure, ask the Holy Spirit for insight into your own heart. Tell God what's troubling you.

3. Now, ask God for wisdom over what's troubling you. What would he have you do, think, or believe today?

James 1:5 says, *"If any of you lacks wisdom, let him ask God, who gives generously to all without reproach, and it will be given him."*

Whenever you need wisdom today, whenever the cares of life grow too great, accept the invitation from God into a place of conversation with him. There is so much more that God can and will do in your life if you'll simply invite him. Don't work, play, or rest without him. Don't live on the leftovers from past spiritual experiences.

Allow conversation to be the gateway to a deeper, more abiding connection with God throughout your day. And watch as conversing with your Creator begins to cause the world in and around you to look on earth as it is in heaven (Matthew 6:10).

My growth tracker S M T W T F S

ACTION

Choose three more times today that you will converse with God. And set an alarm to remind you to take even one minute to converse with God.

If you're interested in more resources on the subject of prayer, check out a phenomenal book on the subject, *The Joy of Listening to God* by Joyce Huggett.

abundance

"I came that they may
have life and have it
abundantly."

JOHN 10:10

A New Bar

1

In week two of *Rhythms*, we're going to focus on rhythms that produce abundant life in and through us.

In John 10:10, Jesus gives this explanation for why he took on flesh for you and me:

> *"The thief comes only to steal and kill and destroy. I came that they may have life and have it abundantly."*

Jesus gives us an opportunity to set a new standard for our lives of abundance, not necessarily in the material sense, but in ways that are much more important.

If you're needing a revitalization of your peace, emotions, and thoughts, and the empowerment to actually take action on those things that truly matter, may God fill you with inward abundance this week as you make space for him to do so.

SCRIPTURE

"I came that they may have life and have it abundantly." —John 10:10

Devotional

We live in an abundant world, created by an abundant God.

God made an Earth brimming with life in seemingly infinite forms, breathed life into humanity, and called it all good. Every morning brings new mercies and new opportunities for love, laughter, healing, wisdom, and action. Every life is made unique, called and equipped to mirror the very nature of Love in whose image we were created.

But somehow, we have settled.

Before Jesus took on flesh, God's people settled for worldly rulers, for the promise of security from godless nations, for idols who were at best an opportunity for drunken celebration. But then Jesus came, and in declaration of his purpose, he spoke these words:

> *The thief comes only to steal and kill and destroy. I came that they may have life and have it abundantly* (John 10:10).

In this moment, Jesus clearly puts his intention for us at odds with the intention of our common enemy. In God alone, we find abundant life. Outside of him, we open ourselves up to theft and destruction.

My life, if I'm honest, is a clear picture of this truth. When I look for purpose, identity, and love outside of the realm of abiding connection in God, I feel as if I'm constantly being robbed. I find myself tempted to give my time to that which serves the incessant needs of others, even at the expense of my relationship with God and those he's given me to love most. I find myself tempted to give my passion to the idols of success, achievement, and affirmation at the expense of having energy left over to simply sit with my two boys, creating memories more valuable than any earthly accolade. I find myself tempted to change who I am for the sake of fitting the mold of whoever is in front of me.

Every time I give in to one of those temptations, my lived experience falls below the standard of abundance Jesus died to bring me.

And maybe the worst part of it all is that somehow I begin to accept a less-than-abundant reality as my new standard for living. I accept that stress is normal, busyness is attached to importance, and productivity is our collective purpose. I lower my bar for living to my own standard, ignoring a dulling sense that life could be about so much more.

But God has a word for you and for me. And that word is: *today*.

Today is a new day.

Today is a fresh chance to raise our bar to the standard of an abundant life. Today is a fresh chance to say no to that which seeks to rob from us, and instead give ourselves fully to that which produces life and fruit in God. Today is a fresh chance to give our time, passion, and purpose to God, ourselves, and others in such a way that when we lie down tonight to rest, we will know that this day truly mattered.

Practically, as we walk through this series called *Rhythms*, here are some rhythms to continue to raise the bar to the standard of abundant life, and actually meet that standard on a daily basis.

Rhythm One: Read the fruits of the Spirit (Gal. 5:22–23) first thing every morning.

Write down the verses and leave the note where you'll see it every day. Allowing the opportunity to experience love, joy, peace, patience, kindness, goodness, faithfulness, gentleness, and self-control to be your new normal drives you to a meaningful time alone with God.

Rhythm Two: Seek to embody abundance.

As a society that almost exclusively values reason, we are failing to recognize the immense truth our intuition and bodies bring us. If you are worn down, not sleeping well, irritable, joyless, and insecure, then something is wrong. Even if reason can't tell you what's off, listen to your body telling you that your life is not abundant, and seek wise counsel from others and wisdom from the Holy Spirit. Practically, begin your time alone with God by closing your eyes, focusing on your breath, and simply paying attention to your physical, emotional, and mental health.

Rhythm Three: Take a true Sabbath every week.

There is no better rhythm for jumping off the proverbial race up the ladder of success than resting from all forms of productivity for one day a week. God himself modeled this for us by resting on the seventh day in the creation story. Scripture commands us often to take and honor a Sabbath (Lev. 23:3). Allow this to be a day when you do no work related to your career or family (budget, grocery shopping, etc.). Instead, set it apart for the remembrance that you are a human being, not a human doing, and that your life is not defined by what you do.

As you find and practice rhythms to raise your bar to the standard of an abundant life in Christ, know that an abundant life doesn't mean you'll always get your way or be healthy, happy, rich, and successful. Abundance is simply living a life from a place of "yes" toward God, and purpose and enjoyment in whatever that "yes" might bring your way.

As we go from a posture of reading to meditation and conversation, may God raise our bar and give us a greater measure of interior abundance in him.

 MEDITATION

Before conversing with God, take a few deep breaths, in and out, in and out, in and out. And slowly close your eyes and simply focus on your breathing.

Take a few moments to listen to your body and take stock of your emotional and mental health. What's causing you stress right now? Is your body feeling normal, or exhibiting symptoms of anxiety or fatigue? Is your mind clear, or swimming with past or possible events?

Rather than correcting or worrying, simply acknowledge how you're doing, and at the same time, how abundantly good your God is.

Rest in the awareness for a few moments.

 CONVERSATION

To help you gather your thoughts and write down what you sense God is saying, grab a journal if you can:

1. Reflect for a few moments on God's bar of abundance for your life. What does that concept and invitation mean to you?

   "I came that they may have life and have it abundantly." —John 10:10

2. What is the main thing holding you back right now from experiencing an abundant life today? Journal your thoughts, ask the Holy Spirit for insight, and seek wisdom over your barriers to abundance.

   "Do not be overcome by evil, but overcome evil with good." —Romans 12:21

3. Raise your bar for today to the standard of abundance and choose right now to say no to anything that would hold you back from reaching it. Surrender any other pursuits at the feet of Jesus, and don't walk away until you have a sense of peace and confidence about your day.

   "My son, give me your heart, and let your eyes observe my ways." —Proverbs 23:26

Don't see this time as an end to your conversation with God today. Allow the Holy Spirit to continue to speak to your heart about whether what's in front of you is an opportunity from him, or a temptation away from the abundance he has for your day.

Obedience to God's command to pray without ceasing is not continuously talking, but continuously listening. In listening to the Spirit, may you have a sense of abiding direction birthed from true connection, and may a growing relationship produce inward abundance that bears more fruit than you thought possible today.

ACTION

Before you go to sleep tonight, take five minutes to journal about your day. What brought you abundant life? What pulled you away from your sense of abundance today? And allow a check-in or examen about your day to be a building block for tomorrow.

"A JOYFUL HEART

IS GOOD MEDICINE,

BUT A CRUSHED SPIRIT

DRIES UP THE BONES."

PROVERBS 17:22

Emotional Abundance

DAY

2

In week two of *Rhythms*, we're going to focus on rhythms that produce abundant life in and through us.

In John 10:10, Jesus gives this explanation for why he took on flesh for you and me:

> *"The thief comes only to steal and kill and destroy. I came that they may have life and have it abundantly."*

Jesus gives us an opportunity to set a new standard for our lives of abundance, not necessarily in the material sense, but in ways that are much more important.

And today, we're looking at how we can experience emotional abundance: embracing, celebrating, and allowing God to move and work fully in the area of our emotions.

SCRIPTURE

"A joyful heart is good medicine, but a crushed spirit dries up the bones." —Proverbs 17:22

Devotional

There is a massive problem facing the Western church, and that problem is the suppression of our emotions. From a young age, particularly in more evangelical Christian circles, we are taught to be skeptical of our emotions. We're taught that anger is a bad emotion, especially at church; conflict is better practiced indirectly or passively; logic and reason are higher and more trustworthy than intuition and feelings.

As a result, we've created a culture that buries emotions, is uncomfortable with the expression of negative feelings, values the creation of façades over the mess that comes with honesty, and leads to burnout and emotional immaturity.

Peter Scazzero, in his book *Emotionally Healthy Spirituality*, describes the problem this way:

> To feel is to be human. To minimize or deny what we feel is a distortion of what it means to be image bearers of God. To the degree that we are unable to express our emotions, we remain impaired in our ability to love God, others, and ourselves well. [3]

Thomas Merton describes the problem this way in *Thoughts in Solitude*:

> The Cross does not sanctify us by destroying human feeling. Detachment is not insensibility. Too many ascetics fail to become great saints precisely because their rules and ascetic practices have **merely deadened their humanity** instead of setting it free to develop richly, in all its capacities, under the influence of grace [emphases added].[4]

We need a revival of values that embraces the full value of the ways God intentionally created us. We need a reprioritization of our senses in a way that values them all equally and holds them all in equal tension so we can be the whole and healthy beings God created us to be. We need to stop suppressing our emotions, and not just the "good ones," so we can allow them to be the clear window into our inner workings they were created to be.

When you're not at peace, then there's something that's causing you unrest, and God wants to shine his light there and bring you healing. When you're angry, there's something at the root of your anger, and whether it be just or unjust, God wants to shine his light there and bring you healing. When you're joyful, there's a seed of the Spirit planted that's bearing fruit, and God wants you to express that joy to the fullest that he might use you to plant a seed of joy in another.

Your emotions are valid. Your emotions are important. You have emotions because God has emotions, and you are beautifully made in his image.

Your emotions are as important as your intellect, logic, and reason. God wants to use your emotions to speak to you, lead you, and work in and through you.

Describing both the problem and opportunity within emotional health, Peter Scazzero also wrote this:

> When we deny our pain, losses, and feelings year after year, we become less and less human. We transform slowly into empty shells with smiley faces painted on them. Sad to say, that is the fruit of much of our discipleship in our churches. But when I began to allow myself to feel a wider range of emotions, including sadness, depression, fear, and anger, a revolution in my spirituality was unleashed. I soon realized that a failure to appreciate the biblical place of feelings within our larger Christian lives has done extensive damage, keeping free people in Christ in slavery.[5]

There is a "revolution in [your] spirituality" available to you today if you will embrace the reality of your emotions, value them as God does, and allow the Spirit to use them to bring to life the full expression of who you are in this moment.

As you move into a time of meditation and conversation, may God meet you powerfully in place of your emotions and lead you to a level of emotional abundance that bears profound fruit in your life, and in the lives of others around you.

MEDITATION

Before conversing with God, take a few deep breaths, in and out, in and out, in and out. And slowly close your eyes and simply focus on your breathing.

Take a few moments and look into your emotions. What emotion are you feeling most in this moment?

Sit with that emotion for a moment, seeking to feel it as fully and consciously as possible. Give it full value, invite the Spirit to be with you fully in the midst of it, and simply rest in awareness of the moment.

CONVERSATION

To help you gather your thoughts and write down what you sense God is saying, grab a journal if you can:

1.   How well do you value your emotions currently? How much do you acknowledge them throughout your day, give them credence, and allow God to speak to you through them?

     "Jesus wept." —John 11:35

2.   What emotion did you sense the most as you made space to meditate and reflect? Take a moment and see your emotion as a window into your inner workings. Why do you think you're feeling that emotion? What perspective, event, person, or belief is at its root?

     "The purpose in a man's heart is like deep water, but a man of understanding will draw it out." —Proverbs 20:5

3.   Raise your bar for today to the standard of abundance and choose right now to give life to your emotions. Ask God for the courage to feel and express your emotions. Ask him to give you insight into how he is speaking, guiding, and working in and

through your emotions today. Take a moment, ask him how deeply he values your emotions, and rest in the revelation he gives you.

"A hot-tempered man stirs up strife, but he who is slow to anger quiets contention." —Proverbs 15:18

One of the most powerful parts of our emotions is how quickly they change, and how often they give us an opportunity to mature and grow to the stature of Christ. Today, if you feel fear for a moment, fully acknowledge it and get revelation through it. Today, if you feel insecurity, fully acknowledge it and allow God to fill you with courage and faith. Today, if you feel joy or love or happiness, express it fully in freedom.

There is untapped power in your emotions, and may today be the day that you journey toward maturity as you seize emotional abundance in God.

My growth tracker S M T W T F S

ACTION

Before you go to sleep, reflect on the chief emotion you experienced today. Set an alarm to remind yourself, and take five minutes, journal in hand, to process that emotion with God. Simply acknowledge it fully, give it full value and credence, and allow the Spirit to speak with you about it.

If you're interested in reading more about the opportunity within emotional health, check out Peter Scazzero's book, *Emotionally Healthy Spirituality*. I could not recommend it more highly.

---

[3] Peter Scazzero, *Emotionally Healthy Spirituality* (Grand Rapids, Michigan: Zondervan, 2006), p. 24.

[4] Thomas Merton, *Thoughts in Solitude* (New York: Farrar, Straus and Giroux, 1999), pg. 2.

[5] Peter Scazzero, pg. 44.

"Set their minds on the

things of the Spirit."

ROMANS 8:5

Abundant Thoughts

3

In week two of *Rhythms*, we're going to focus on rhythms that produce abundant life in and through us.

In John 10:10, Jesus gives this explanation for why he took on flesh for you and me:

> *"The thief comes only to steal and kill and destroy. I came that they may have life and have it abundantly."*

Jesus gives us an opportunity to set a new standard for our lives of abundance, not necessarily in the material sense, but in those ways much more important.

And today, we're looking at how we can have abundant thoughts, allowing the Spirit to work in our minds to give us true, biblical perspectives on ourselves and the world around us.

May we discover lies we've believed that are wrecking our sense of an abundant life today. And may God replace those lies with truth that bears fruit greater than we could have imagined.

SCRIPTURE

"Those who live according to the Spirit set their minds on the things of the Spirit."
—Romans 8:5

Devotional

The battle for a peaceful, gospel-centered mind is one waged, for me, so far in the background that often I forget it's even going on. And yet, when I remember to glimpse into the war over my thoughts, even for a moment, I can see so clearly the impact this battle has on my lived experience every day.

For example, recently I've been struggling with insecurity. Some days I wake up and wonder how I, with my weaknesses, failures, and faults, could ever have ended up where I am today. How could I ever be good enough, capable enough, talented enough to love and guide my family well, love and guide believers well, and love and obey this God who is so worthy of my full devotion?

When I peer into the reality of my insecurities, I realize the havoc this battle for humble confidence is having on my life.

And while the number of mental battles occurring in my life in this season are far too great to walk through now, the reality of those battles, I believe, is true for all of us.

If you were to stop, even for a moment, right now, and peer into your own mind, what war is being waged? Where are you wrestling with thoughts that are having a negative impact on your life? To put it plainly, what lies are you believing that are robbing you of a greater measure of abundant life?

Your mind is the gateway to the rest of your being. How you think is how you feel. What you come to believe is what will guide you. Your assumptions, true or untrue, checked or unchecked, color every experience you will have.

Fyodor Dostoevsky said it this way:

> There are things which a man is afraid to tell even to himself, and every decent man has a number of such things stored away in his mind.

While that reality sounds, and is, daunting, there is also an immense opportunity inside of the battle for mental health and for mental abundance. And the opportunity lies in the fact that we have a commander with us at all times in the Spirit, who yearns to guide us to a place of strength and victory in the place of our thoughts.

Romans 12:2 says, *"Do not be conformed to this world, but be transformed by the renewal of your mind, that by testing you may discern what is the will of God, what is good and acceptable and perfect."* Inside this verse is a promise: your mind can be renewed. The battle over your thoughts can be won. Lies can be disowned. That which is good, acceptable, and perfect can be yours if you will submit your mind for transformation in God.

To illustrate the power of this promise of God, I have been clinging to Isaiah 26:3 in this past season:

> *You keep him in perfect peace whose mind is stayed on you, because he trusts in you.*

In our society, stress has become our new normal. There is a wealth of research and data that proves we are living in an epidemic of anxiety and stress, and it's not getting better. But if we as God's children will *"stay"* our minds on God with trust in our hearts, we can have *"perfect peace."*

And if I need anything today, I need perfect peace.

So how do we move from our current ways of thinking to the reality of having an abundant thought life?

As we're in this series on rhythms, today I want to suggest a few ways that you can experience greater mental abundance every day.

Rhythm One: Submit your mind to God every day in your devotional time.

Rather than coming to First15, or whatever resources you use, with a closed mind, thinking that your current reality is just how it is, come with an open mind, believing that God can do mighty things in your mind, even in fifteen minutes.

Rhythm Two: Listen to your body.

Our body responds to the way we're thinking. When we're afraid, our body feels it. When we're insecure, our body responds. When we're stressed, anxious, rushed, or unsure, our body can let us know. We need to begin to value the insight our physiology provides us rather than rationalizing ourselves out of an opportunity to invite God to do meaningful work in our minds.

Rhythm Three: Write down your thoughts honestly, every day, without reservation or judgment.

A journal can be a powerful partner in taking our thoughts captive (2 Corinthians 10:5). If you will write down what you're thinking and how it makes you feel, and get it out as honestly as you can, you'll be able to see your thoughts for what they actually are. And in engaging in that process, you might discover what's truly at the root of your ways of thinking. That place of honesty is where God can do his most transformative work.

Right now, as we move into a time of meditation and conversation, believe that God can transform your mind today. You can find victory over thoughts that are robbing you of an abundant life today. You can find peace as the Spirit meets you in the place of your thinking and brings you personal, transformative truth.

 MEDITATION

Before conversing with God, take a few deep breaths, in and out, in and out, in and out. And slowly close your eyes and simply focus on your breathing.

Take a few moments and look into your thoughts. What belief, lie, or thought is robbing you of an abundant life the most right now?

Fully acknowledge the thought, sit with it, and invite the Spirit to meet you as you hold that thought with full honesty and humility.

To help you gather your thoughts and write down what you sense God is saying, grab a journal if you can:

1. Process a thought that's robbing you of an abundant life the most. What is the thought? Where does it come from? How does it affect you? Process on paper the reality of your thoughts as honestly as possible without fear or judgment.

    "We destroy arguments and every lofty opinion raised against the knowledge of God, and take every thought captive to obey Christ." —2 Corinthians 10:5

2. Look for a verse that speaks to your thoughts and reflect on it. Scripture is a powerful ally in the war for mental abundance.

    "Finally, brothers, whatever is true, whatever is honorable, whatever is just, whatever is pure, whatever is lovely, whatever is commendable, if there is any excellence, if there is anything worthy of praise, think about these things." —Philippians 4:8

3. Invite the Spirit into the area of your thinking and seek to raise the bar of your thoughts to the measure of abundance. Ask God for revelation on your thinking; ask him to illuminate a path to victory. Reframe the thought in light of his truth and take a few moments to rest in new revelation.

    "Set your minds on things that are above, not on things that are on earth." —Colossians 3:2

Every day with First15, you'll have an opportunity to take your thoughts captive. If you'll allow it, this rhythm can be a way to begin every day in a position of mental strength.

But this rhythm will only be powerful if you come to it with honesty and faith.

If you believe that God can transform your thoughts, and speak to you directly, and you make real space for him to do so, then he will.

As you move into a position of action for your day, take stock of whether or not you feel more strengthened in your mind. As you go about your day, reflect on how that position of strength changes your lived experience today.

ACTION

One of the most powerful ways to shine light, and receive healing, is to give visibility to your thoughts through real communication. So, today, choose one person you trust to communicate your thought life to. If you want feedback, ask them for it. If you just need someone to talk to, tell them before you share that you just need someone to listen without judgment or response.

If you need deeper help in the area of your thought life, I truly want to encourage you to find a licensed Christian counselor or therapist. Conversing with someone trained to help you discover the root of your way of thinking, and serve as a guide to finding healing, is an incredibly valuable resource. I love going to counseling. It has been incredibly healing in my life, and I believe it's an untapped resource we as believers should more readily access.

"One who waters will

himself be watered."

PROVERBS 11:25

Living Generously

4

In week two of *Rhythms*, we're going to focus on rhythms that produce abundant life in and through us.

In John 10:10, Jesus gives this explanation for why he took on flesh for you and me:

> *"The thief comes only to steal and kill and destroy. I came that they may have life and have it abundantly."*

Jesus gives us an opportunity to set a new standard for our lives of abundance, not necessarily in the material sense, but in ways that are much more important.

And today, we're looking at how living generously with our words, assumptions, and actions can not only bring a greater measure of abundant life to others, but to ourselves as well.

SCRIPTURE

"Whoever brings blessing will be enriched, and one who waters will himself be watered." —Proverbs 11:25

Devotional

As hard as I try to orient my life around the principles of my faith, every day I seem to struggle with this one foundational teaching of Jesus:

"Whoever loses his life for my sake will find it." —Matthew 16:25b

Every day I wake up and I have to pry my pride from my fists and lay it down at the feet of Jesus. No matter how deeply I pursue humility, how deeply I seek to remove myself from the center of my own story and place God there instead, every day the cycle of surrender begins again.

At its core, I believe that generosity is simply losing our "me-centric" mentality, that we find a life of beauty that's only experienced when God is at the center of our stories.

There are some teachers of the faith, teachers I love, who position generosity as a key to unlock the abundance of God. And while I do believe that sometimes, oftentimes, we have to practice our way into honest belief, I also believe generosity, in its purest form, is meant to be an expression of worship birthed from a place of genuine love and humility.

Generosity is the natural overflow when we realize that you and I already have everything we could ever need, and everything we could honestly want, in God. Generosity is the natural overflow when our hearts grow to more naturally pray the beautiful words of David in Psalm 23:

> The LORD is my shepherd; I shall not want.

Generosity is the fruit of the realization that we have already been given a life of abundance in God, salvation, love, peace, and relationship, those gifts that can be opened at any moment, in the midst of any trial or tribulation—gifts whose goodness is inherent and transcends the ups and downs of this life.

As we're in this series on rhythms of abundance, today we have the opportunity to accept an invitation to a deeper level of satiation in God. But accepting the invitation to foundational satisfaction in God comes with one ask: that we would leave our notions of abundance at the door and set our eyes only on the better blessing that's sitting at the feet of Jesus.

When we've surrendered again, we'll find that generosity is the very heartbeat of action that God calls us to. Generosity is the vehicle by which we see Jesus's prayer fulfilled: that it would be *on earth as it is in heaven*" (Matthew 6:10). Generosity is the posture our hearts are meant to take naturally, to say that from the place of satisfaction and identity in God, you can have all of me.

Generous living is not obligatory living, not saying "yes" when our hearts cry "no," but honest acts of love that shine God's brilliant light to even the darkest corners of the human heart.

John MacArthur, when describing generosity, wrote these words:

> God made all of His creation to give. He made the sun, the moon, the stars, the clouds, the earth, the plants to give. He also designed His supreme creation, man, to give. But fallen man is the most reluctant giver in all of God's creation.[6]

In living a life of generosity, you will find it impossible to outgive what God will bring back to you. You will find it impossible to give more delight, more purpose, more love, and more life than you will experience in God as your life is molded and shaped into a purer likeness of Jesus.

Before we make space to meditate and have conversation with God about living a life of generosity, I want to recommend three practices I believe can be a part of your regular rhythm of life to help you uncover the generous spirit God has already placed within you.

Rhythm One: Surrender your pride to God every day, first thing.

With the First15 app, if this daily devotional is your daily guide to God's presence, we give you a tool by which you can lay your pride down at the feet of Jesus every day. Especially if you take time to worship with us every day, use that time to remove yourself from the center of your story and place God there instead.

Rhythm Two: As you empty your hands in surrender, allow God to fill them.

It's incredibly difficult to live generously when we feel that we're losing more in life than we're receiving. It will be near impossible to live generously if you do not make space every day to receive the abundant blessing of God. You must first receive his peace, love, purpose, identity, and then follow his lead through the doors he is opening.

Rhythm Three: Give your time, talent, and treasure away freely.

Corrie ten Boom said:

"The measure of a life, after all, is not its duration, but its donation."

You only have one life to live here on this earth, and your purpose is not fulfilled through how much of yourself and your resources you keep to yourself. It's in giving as much of yourself away every day that you can—your time, talent, and treasure—that you will discover the abundant life that only comes through wholehearted devotion.

As you make space to meditate and have conversation with God, come to him openhanded and allow him to show you what's in the way of generous living. Choose faith and heavenly purpose today in his presence and allow God to bring to life a genuine desire for living generously.

[6] John MacArthur, *The MacArthur New Testament Commentary: 1 Corinthians* (Chicago: Moody Publishers, 1984), pg. 456.

Before conversing with God, take a few deep breaths, in and out, in and out, in and out. And slowly close your eyes and simply focus on being present in this moment.

Now reflect on these words of Scripture, allowing them to sink from your head to your heart:

> *"For where your treasure is, there your heart will be also."* —Matthew 6:21

Maintain a posture of reflection for a few moments.

CONVERSATION

To help you gather your thoughts and write down what you sense God is saying, grab a journal if you can:

1. Take time to lay down your pride at the feet of Jesus. Process ways in which you are living as the center of your own story and surrender them to God.

   "For whoever would save his life will lose it, but whoever loses his life for my sake will find it." —Matthew 16:25

2. What is most in the way of your ability to live generously? Ask the Holy Spirit for insight and maintain a posture of reflection for a few moments.

3. How can you live most generously today in a way that is honest and true? Ask God for insight into how he is calling you toward generosity, and who he is asking you to be generous with.

   "They are to do good, to be rich in good works, to be generous and ready to share, thus storing up treasure for themselves as a good foundation for the future, so that they may take hold of that which is truly life." —1 Timothy 6:18–19

As you move to a posture of action today, remember that Jesus radically shifted the notion of generosity in observation of the widow giving a mite in worship. In stark contrast to giving of greater financial worth, Jesus said, *"Truly, I tell you, this poor widow has put in more than all of them"* (Luke 21:3).

Don't judge your generosity by the measurements of the world today, but by the depth of your obedience and love.

My growth tracker   S M T W T F S

ACTION

There are seemingly infinite ways you can demonstrate generosity today. Perhaps the most transformative might be to choose to be generous with your assumptions of others. Rather than assuming the worst of others, or assuming that you know the heart behind their words or actions, choose to assume the best.

The old principle rings true: We judge others by their actions, but ourselves by our intentions.

If there is someone you regularly interact with, maybe a spouse or coworker, whom you're struggling to love right now, give space for your heart to be genuinely loving toward them today by choosing generous assumptions.

And allow a more positive outlook toward others to spur you to greater actions of generosity.

"DO NOT BE ANXIOUS."

PHILIPPIANS 4:6

Abundant Moments

DAY

5

In week two of *Rhythms*, we're going to focus on rhythms that produce abundant life in and through us.

In John 10:10, Jesus gives this explanation for why he took on flesh for you and me:

> *"The thief comes only to steal and kill and destroy. I came that they may have life and have it abundantly."*

Jesus gives us an opportunity to set a new standard for our lives of abundance, not necessarily in the material sense, but in ways that are much more important.

And today, we're looking at how being fully present, simply living in this moment, empowers us to soak up far more of the abundant life God is providing for us than dwelling in the past or worrying over the future.

SCRIPTURE

"Do not be anxious about anything, but in everything by prayer and supplication with thanksgiving let your requests be made known to God." —Philippians 4:6

Devotional

Across the past couple of years, one spiritual discipline has stood out to me as the key that unlocks the greatest depths of abundant life: the practice of being present.

As simple as the discipline sounds, it requires daily commitment, a heart filled with trust in God, and a constant refusal of the values and rewards of our societies.

First, let's look at the biblical and experiential truths around the power of being present. Then, let's look at how we, even in our use of a daily devotional like First15, can develop our ability to more fully dwell in the present moment— heart, mind, and soul.

In my experience with Christian teaching, the concept of being present isn't really being taught or even talked about. We somehow have put most or all of our collective hopes and dreams in the life that is to come and have focused on a singular objective of getting as many souls to heaven instead of seeking to bring heaven to earth as fully as possible in every moment of every day.

And in doing so, I actually believe we've taken on some of the responsibility that only God can own and we've given away some of the most important responsibilities he's given us to own here in this life.

For example, I have often heard believers disregard our first job of stewarding the earth and its resources, putting our hope of a healthy planet in the concept of a new heaven and new earth. I see Christians working their fingers to the bone in their "calling" while forgoing our most basic purpose of simply sitting at Jesus's feet in love, loving ourselves as he does, and caring for our most intimate relationships, such as our spouses or children.

We have somehow, as a people, gotten our priorities reversed. Rather than allowing our work to be the overflow of loving relationships, we prioritize work and give our relationships what's left over. And slowly but surely, I believe our priorities, as made evident through our actions, are proclaiming a gospel of works, not of grace.

In many ways, maybe even most ways, I believe the antidote to this problem of reversed priorities is following the words of David in Psalm 46:10:

> *"Be still, and know that I am God.*
> *I will be exalted among the nations,*
> *I will be exalted in the earth!"*

The best way for us to come to a place of faith that at the end of it all, God will be exalted, is not with action, but in stillness. Stillness is perhaps the greatest act of faith you and I can possibly muster. In stillness, we declare that God is God, and we are not. In stillness, we declare that the kingdom is God's to advance, and we simply have our unique role to play. In stillness, we find the peace and hope that empowers us to communicate the gospel from a place of rest, instead of from a place of self-sufficiency.

You see, while God is eternal and dwells in all of time and history, he specifically made us without that ability. All we have is this moment. The past is the past. The future is not promised to us. The greatest strategic minds, the greatest planners and thinkers cannot predict what will happen tomorrow.

As hard as we try and fail to create the future in the image of our purposes and plans, in worrying over it, we fail to grab hold of the abundant life God is providing for us that can only be experienced while being fully present in this moment.

In Matthew 6:34, Jesus says:

> *"Therefore do not be anxious about tomorrow, for tomorrow will be anxious for itself. Sufficient for the day is its own trouble."*

The pathway to building the better tomorrow that you want for yourself and for others is in abiding fully in God today. The pathway to greater love and action is in soaking up all of God's loving power there is in this moment. The way to walk through the doors we wish would open for us is to look for the doors God is opening right now, and to practice faithful obedience right where we are.

Every moment is brimming with opportunity. In every moment, wherever God is at work, there is exponential opportunity for miracles, transformation, and love. But to say yes to those opportunities, we have to be present with ourselves, be present with the Spirit, and be present in empathy and compassion for those God has placed around us in this moment.

So, as we look to become more present in the moment, to dwell and abide more fully with God right where and when we are, I want to unpack a rhythm already built within First15 to help you practice being present.

Rhythm: Practice Christian meditation.

Meditation, especially in Christian circles, has become a taboo concept. We associate meditation only with Eastern religions and, in doing so, fail to grab hold of a biblical and historical Christian practice.

Psalm 1:2–3 says, *"But his delight is in the law of the LORD, and on his law he meditates day and night. He is like a tree planted by streams of water that yields its fruit in its season, and its leaf does not wither. In all that he does, he prospers."*

Isaiah 26:3 says, *"You keep him in perfect peace whose mind is stayed on you, because he trusts in you."*

Scripture is actually filled with exhortations to meditate. And for centuries, Christian leaders have looked to the practice of meditation to take Scripture from the head to the heart, to make space to hear from God and be transformed, and to lay down that which is peripheral in our faith to better take hold of that which is essential.

Every day with First15, you have the opportunity to make space for God to fill you through meditation. While it's tempting to brush past meditation to get to those practices that are more measurable, which seem more actionable, it's possible that what we need most is not more information, more conversation, or more action, but simply more stillness and silence.

So, as you come to First15, however often you use it as a resource to grow closer to God, give as much time and focus to the time of meditation as you can muster. Watch as daily stillness and silence deepen your experience of God and transform you in ways beyond words into a purer expression of his likeness.

MEDITATION

Before conversing with God, take a few deep breaths, in and out, in and out, in and out. And slowly close your eyes and simply focus on being present in this moment.

Lay all your anxieties, all your tasks and projects, your past and your future at the feet of your omnipotent and omnipresent God, and simply be with him.

If your mind wanders, gently return your focus back to God. Allow Psalm 46:10, and God's promise of exaltation in the nations, to be a guide to authentic connection and trust in him today:

> *"Be still, and know that I am God. I will be exalted among the nations, I will be exalted in the earth!"*

Hold your posture of stillness and silence as long as you can.

CONVERSATION

To help you gather your thoughts and write down what you sense God is saying, grab a journal if you can:

1. What is your experience like when you're still and silent before the Lord? Write down the thoughts, feelings, and beliefs you experience.

2. What is most at odds with your ability to live in the present moment? Do you dwell most often on the past or future? And what's behind the temptation that pulls you away from the moment?

   "Worry does not empty tomorrow of its sorrow. It empties today of its strength." —Corrie ten Boom

3. What positive effects would you experience if you could be more present in the world around you? How would it benefit you to be more present with God, with yourself, and with others throughout your day?

   "And which of you by being anxious can add a single hour to his span of life?" —Matthew 6:27

As you move to a posture of action today, ask the Holy Spirit to draw you to the present when your mind inevitably wanders. Trust God with the weight of the future and ask him to empower you to make the biggest impact you can in the present. Trust God with what tomorrow will bring, and pour your heart, soul, mind, and strength into the path he is illuminating before you today.

Choose today to look where God is at work and join him there with faith that even one day's work can bear fruit into eternity.

You were made, uniquely wired for something special today. Grab hold of the life that is in front of you in this moment and experience the abundance that comes from soaking up all of God's goodness there is right here, and right now.

My growth tracker S M T W T F S

ACTION

Make time today to be fully present with someone you love for twenty minutes. Instead of working together on a project, or consuming entertainment, or being in the same room but focusing on social media, simply be together and enjoy meaningful conversation.

Ask good questions, like about how they're feeling, or what they're thinking, or what they're most enjoying in life right now. And really listen. Enjoy the abundance that comes from a time of focused connection with someone and soak up all of the goodness in those moments that you can.

"Outdo one

another in

showing honor."

ROMANS 12:10

Abundant Relationships

6

In week two of Rhythms, we're going to focus on rhythms that produce abundant life in and through us.

In John 10:10, Jesus gives this explanation for why he took on flesh for you and me:

> *"The thief comes only to steal and kill and destroy. I came that they may have life and have it abundantly."*

Jesus gives us an opportunity to set a new standard for our lives of abundance, not necessarily in the material sense, but in those ways much more important.

And today, we're going to explore how God provides leadership down a pathway to having abundant relationships, if we'll simply be willing to follow.

SCRIPTURE

"Outdo one another in showing honor." —Romans 12:10

Devotional

In a society that defines our value by what we do, it can be incredibly difficult to invest the time and energy it takes to develop meaningful relationships. When productivity is the measure of our worth, people will inevitably end up becoming a means to greater productivity and results. We give work, paid or unpaid, the best of ourselves, and relationships unrelated to work oftentimes get what's left over.

And hear me say: we were created to work. Work is not a symptom of the fall. Work is a beautiful gift from God.

But as a society, we've built our value systems backward. And slowly it's eating away at the purpose for which we were created, and the opportunities that will produce the kind of living that most glorifies God and satisfies us.

Plain and simple, abundant living is all about relationships. Simply look at most of the wealthy to see that money alone does not satisfy. Simply look at many of the famous to see that recognition does not produce happiness. Simply look at the rate of burnout among faith leaders to see that doing

"God's work" is not enough to sustain us. Simply look at the rate of exodus from the faith among young believers, about 1 million a year below the age of thirty, to see that no matter what we proclaim or how we proclaim it, what is attractive about our faith is our manner of being, not of doing.

We need a revival of relationships. We need a restoration of values that says we're human beings, not human doings. And that revival must take place first in the heart. It must be lived, be authentic, and be easily perceived among others around us.

Think about your own life for a moment. What actually satisfies you? When do you feel that you're being most like who you were created to be? When do you most feel God's pleasure over you?

For me, as a goal-oriented individual, I find it's actually the recognition from my peers that excites me about producing results. I find that finances excite me when I have the opportunity to give gifts to my two boys and my wife, or to create an experience for the family. I find that what I love most about church isn't the production, but the way it helps me connect with God, myself, and others.

John writes in 1 John 2:17 these prophetic words:

> And the world is passing away along with its desires, but whoever does the will of God abides forever.

And what is the will of God? Paul writes in Galatians 5:14: *"For the whole law is fulfilled in one word: 'You shall love your neighbor as yourself.'"* And in context Jesus tells us, *"You shall love the Lord your God with all your heart and with all your soul and with all your mind. This is the great and first commandment. And a second is like it: You shall love your neighbor as yourself"* (Matthew 22:37–39).

God's will is simply that we would love: love him, love ourselves, and love others.

If the hours we spend aren't toward that end, they are wasted. If the passion and resources we invest in a career, friendship, project, or opportunity aren't for love, they are wasted. Abundant life is that simple, and that challenging.

So, in this series on rhythms, what rhythms are available to us to reorient our life around loving relationships, and how can we practice those rhythms well to invest our whole being in what matters most?

Today, I want to explore a rhythm around each relationship God calls us to: our relationship with him, ourselves, and others.

Rhythm One: Give God dedicated time alone every day.

Rick Warren said, "The best use of life is love. The best expression of love is time. The best time to love is now." Our time is our most valuable resource. The best place to start in developing a loving, thriving relationship with God is to give him our time every morning, first thing. We created First15 explicitly for this purpose, but whatever resource you use, I truly believe the most important thing you can do every day is to begin your day alone in God's presence.

Rhythm Two: Journal every day.

There are amazing studies in both the sacred and secular spaces around the benefits of journaling. Loving yourself well begins with self-awareness. I believe the best way to become self-aware is to journal every day.

Practically, if you can spend time journaling in the conversation time with First15, or at the beginning of your day to discover how you're doing, beginning with self-discovery is the first step you need to take to love yourself well.

If you're feeling stressed, or insecure, or overflowing with joy, journal about it. And watch as the Spirit helps you to love yourself as he does.

Rhythm Three: Ask good questions and listen well.

Perhaps the most loving thing we can do with others around us is to ask good questions of them and listen well. When we engage people in meaningful conversation, free of judgment or even advice, we become a safe space for them to be known and therefore to be truly loved.

So, when you're with someone today, choose to be undistracted by technology or thinking toward what's coming next, and be as present with that person as you can possibly be.

As we move now into a time of meditation and conversation, choose to lay down your value of productivity and the ways and system of your society, and pick up God's values, God's ways, and God's systems.

Before conversing with God, take a few deep breaths, in and out, in and out, in and out. And slowly close your eyes and simply focus on being present in this moment.

Reflect in stillness and silence about what life would look like if loving relationships were your singular driver.

If your mind wanders, gently return your focus back to God.

Hold your posture of stillness and silence as long as you can.

CONVERSATION

To help you gather your thoughts and write down what you sense God is saying, grab a journal if you can:

1. What priorities do you have about loving relationships? What is driving you right now that doesn't align with God's value system of loving relationships?

2. Take time to confess those wrong priorities to God and receive his loving forgiveness. Rest in his presence.

3. How can you best love God, love yourself, and love another today? Write down one practical step you will take to invest in each relationship today.

As you move to a posture of action today, ask the Holy Spirit to convict you whenever you begin to give your focus, passion, and resources to something other than loving relationships.

Look for opportunities to love God well today, to worship him and give him thanks and glory.

Listen to your body today, when it's telling you that you're stressed, worried, or tired. Look for an opportunity to take better care of yourself today.

Look for a person who needs love today and ask the Holy Spirit for insight into how to love them well. Choose to be courageous and to love another even if it costs you a moment of productivity or an opportunity for personal gain.

ACTION

Share the practical step you're going to take today to love God, love yourself, and love another with someone you trust. Ask them to hold you accountable to following through on investing your day into what matters most: loving relationships.

May you feel your spirit lifted today as you orient your life around the purposes and plans of God. And may you experience the power of action actually driving you toward a place of abiding in God, rather than away from a sense of connection with him.

"Whoever abides in me

and I in him."

JOHN 15:5

Abundant Fruit

7

In week two of Rhythms, we're going to focus on rhythms that produce abundant life in and through us.

In John 10:10, Jesus gives this explanation for why he took on flesh for you and me:

> *"The thief comes only to steal and kill and destroy. I came that they may have life and have it abundantly."*

Jesus gives us an opportunity to set a new standard for our lives of abundance, not necessarily in the material sense, but in ways that are much more important.

And today, we're going to explore how in an abiding relationship with God, we will naturally produce abundant and eternal fruit.

"Whoever abides in me and I in him, he it is that bears much fruit, for apart from me you can do nothing." —John 15:5b

Devotional

As we close this series on rhythms of abundance, today we're going to look at how true abundant living always produces abundant fruit.

Lately when I've been hearing sermons or reading books that deal with the topic of action, I find myself significantly put off by most of the content. Words and ideas that used to motivate me, to push me forward to action, now seem to push me further from it.

Across the last two years, the deepest work God has done in me deals with the subject of motivation. Am I motivated by pleasing people or loving people? Am I driven to the production of results for my glory or for the satisfaction of the God I love? Are my works birthed from a gospel of grace or actions?

Am I working from a place of already abiding in God, or to earn my way into the upper echelons of a hierarchical kingdom?

As a believer, with confidence in the reality of heaven, the verses that terrify me the most don't have to do with judgment, or even heaven or hell. The verse that terrifies me the most comes from Jesus in John 15:5:

> *Whoever abides in me and I in him, he it is that bears much fruit, for apart from me you can do nothing.*

Jesus doesn't say that apart from abiding in him, you can't put in maximum effort or work your fingers to the bone. But he does say that apart from him, *"you can do nothing."*

Unless our work is done from a place of abiding, it will produce nothing. Unless our work is done out of love, we are a *"noisy gong or a clanging cymbal"* (1 Corinthians 13:1).

But Scripture also tells us that faith and works are inherently linked. James 2:26 says, *"For as the body apart from the spirit is dead, so also faith apart from works is dead."*

My point for us today is simply this: if we focus primarily on the production of fruit and works, they possibly and even likely will be meaningless, regardless of the worldly recognition and applause. But if we focus on vibrant faith, on abiding connection with God, we are promised the production of good fruit with eternal impact.

A vinedresser does not focus his attention on the grape itself. He focuses his attention on the care of the vine and its branches, knowing and believing that a healthy vine produces good fruit.

So today, if you're concerned about the abundance of fruit from your life, don't look first to your hands, but to your heart. Don't attempt to muster up energy and action, but invest in the soil of your heart. Be still before the Lord, wait on him, and do the deeper work of connecting with God's love in an authentic, transcendent way.

The world needs what you were created to be more than it needs what you can do in your own strength. Lay down the praise and approval of your peers, choose faithful obedience in love, and trust God with the results of your life.

As we move to a time of meditation, make space in your heart for God to fill with his loving presence. Allow his nearness to soften your heart, to empower you to take his kingdom off your shoulders, and to seek abiding connection above all else.

MEDITATION

Before conversing with God, take a few deep breaths, in and out, in and out, in and out. And slowly close your eyes and simply focus on being present in this moment.

Allow yourself to notice your perspective and relationship with bearing fruit. Where do you feel joy? Where do you feel pressure? What would you like God to speak into today?

CONVERSATION

To help you gather your thoughts and write down what you sense God is saying, grab a journal if you can:

1. When was a time that bearing fruit felt natural and filled with joy? What was happening in your life and in your being that contributed to those moments?

2. Where do you feel shame or pressure over bearing fruit? Knowing that shame doesn't come from God, where do you think the shame might be coming from?

3. What's one way you can naturally and joyfully bear fruit today?

The advancing of God's kingdom is not on your shoulders. Your job is to stay close to God, stay healthy in God, and say "yes" to where he is leading you. Some days that leadership might feel truly significant in your own eyes. Some days it might feel easy and natural.

The specific fruit and amount of fruit you bear is not up to you. It's up to God. Stay connected to your vine and bear whatever comes, knowing that God has you and your world in his hands.

ACTION

What's one practical step you can take today to say "yes" to bearing the fruit God is raising up within you?

Write that step down and post it somewhere you'll see it. Enjoy the experience of partnering with God in bringing his kingdom to earth today.

healing

"Bless the LORD,

O my soul."

PSALM 103:2

A Healing God

1

In week three of *Rhythms*, we're looking at rhythms that help us make space for the daily healing we need.

The rigors of daily life, not even including the tougher seasons we all experience, seem to leave us battered and bruised in one way or another. Whether it's exhaustion, emotional hurts, or the physical effects of stress and anxiety, we desperately need to discover how to receive the healing our good God longs to give.

May we find rhythms each day this week that prepare us, mind, body, and soul, to receive continual healing.

SCRIPTURE

"Bless the LORD, O my soul, and forget not all his benefits, who forgives all your iniquity, who heals all your diseases, who redeems your life from the pit, who crowns you with steadfast love and mercy." —Psalm 103:2–4

Devotional

As we begin a new week, looking at how we can create rhythms to receive the daily healing we so desperately need, I want to begin by simply looking at the healing nature of our God.

When I bring up the word or concept of *healing* in Christian circles, I normally experience a great divide. There are those in our faith I truly love who believe wholeheartedly that God's intention is always to heal, that any iniquity or emotional or physical wound is outside of God's will, and it's our duty to partner with him in seeing them healed.

There are also believers I love and respect who do not believe that God works supernaturally or disruptively toward the direct healing of wounds. They see pain as something God either allows or intends for the growth and development of us as a people.

My goal today is not to align myself or First15 with a certain perspective or group in regard to healing, but rather to acknowledge that Scripture and our human experience are clear that healing is both good and necessary. In order to receive the healing that is available to us, we need to develop rhythms to our life that invite and accept it.

My belief is that if we open our eyes and look a bit more broadly, we'll see a world created on the basis of rejuvenation. The seasons represent birth, life, and death as a yearly reminder that there is goodness in the process, even those parts that appear less beautiful or fruitful. To grow food, our land must be cultivated, seeds must be planted, life must spring forth, and the fruit of that growth must be gathered and prepared and consumed.

Every living thing requires rest and rejuvenation to continue to produce and create.

But in a society that demands constant productivity, I fear that we're forgoing those rhythms of rejuvenation that are both good in and of themselves and necessary to actually engage in the good works we were created for. In a society where rest is considered lazy and enjoyment of life is at best nonessential and at worst frivolous, we're creating more rhythms in attempt to squeeze out even more fruit while disregarding what perhaps is the more foundational half of our chief end: "to glorify God, **and to enjoy him forever.**"

My point for us today is this: We serve a healing God that longs for our whole being to be restored. But like all good gifts, including salvation, that gift of healing must be received.

To receive the healing that comes from true, deep rest, we have to create rhythms for sleep that posture us to receive all the amazing fruits that come from continual full nights of rejuvenation. To receive emotional healing, we cannot disregard both the deep-seated emotional wounds from our childhood, as well as the daily emotional wounds that happen from doing life with imperfect people. To receive physical healing, we cannot disregard when our body is telling us that it's worn down or exhausted; we cannot simply push through sickness and pain. We have to make space to rest, get the care and attention we need, and give credence to our body's ability to tell us what we need.

To fully embody who God has created us to be, we need a radical reversal of values. We need to fully align our beliefs, actions, focus, and time with the principles of a God who, without weakness, chose to rest as the final act of creation, rather than the world that tells us we will be happy if we only had and did a little bit more.

So, as we move to a time of meditation and conversation, I want to encourage you to reorient your attention and time with three rhythms in mind:

Rhythm One: Get a full night's sleep every night.

The science of sleep is absolutely shocking. God created us to need sleep not as a defect, but because rest and sleep are inherently good. If you do nothing else to make space for the healing you need, choose to get a full night's sleep.

Rhythm Two: Value your emotions by making time every day to process them.

The conversation part of First15 is a great way to begin your day processing your emotions in the context of God's presence. Don't allow emotional wounds to fester. The longer we let them go unhealed, the more damage they do to us and others. And if you need a safe space and person to process your wounds with, I want to encourage you to find a licensed counselor or therapist. God wants healing for your emotions, but healing only comes when you see your wounds for what they are and accept God's truth and love.

Rhythm Three: Listen to what your body is telling you.

Our bodies are powerful tools to let us know how we're doing. If you feel unsettled and restless, maybe you need to get up and exert some energy. If you feel weary and worn down, maybe there's something going on in your life that's causing you more stress or pain than you know. Is your mind racing and troubled? If so, maybe you need to journal to get to the bottom of whatever is capturing your attention. Your body is not bad, and your soul is good. You are a whole being with valuable information being processed through your body that you might not fully understand. That's an invitation to receive the gift of God's healing.

As we move now to a time of meditation and conversation, where do you need healing today? What is bothering you most, pulling life out of you, a place where God wants to give you the gift of healing if you'll simply make the space to receive it?

Go to God with that need today and watch him work.

 MEDITATION

Before conversing with God, take a few deep breaths, in and out, in and out, in and out. And slowly close your eyes and simply focus on being present in this moment.

Take some time in the stillness to increase your awareness of how you're doing. Find one place you want to bring to God for healing today and sit with it for a moment.

Look at the wound or need from multiple angles, allow the Holy Spirit to bring revelation of what is going on at a deeper level, and prepare your heart and mind for God to speak and work.

 CONVERSATION

To help you gather your thoughts and write down what you sense God is saying, grab a journal if you can:

1. Write down your thoughts about your area of need. Where did the need come from? What effects has it had on you? Are you seeing it as truthfully as you can, or operating based on assumption?

2. Ask God to speak truth over your area of need. Find Scripture that relates to the need. Ask the Holy Spirit for insight and wisdom. And rest in revelation for a moment.

3. Ask God to illuminate the path to healing. If you desire to, ask God for healing right now. If you believe it will take more time, write down the steps you believe you need to get full healing. Ask God for the courage and faith to commit to those steps together.

While investing in your healing does take time and focus, it's an investment that will produce exponential results in your life. There's no better way to proclaim the true and full gospel than demonstrating an abundant, healed lifestyle. There's no better way to love others than to come to a place of healing yourself, that you might love them with the fullest expression of who you were created to be when operating in health.

Taking the time to be continually rejuvenated and healed is not a selfish endeavor, but a selfless endeavor that brings God glory and bears fruit in your life and the lives of others around you.

So, as we focus on healing this week, know that God longs to meet you in power every day and guide you down that path to continual rejuvenation and healing in him.

ACTION

Write down the path to healing that you need most today, and if you're able, share it with someone you're close to.

If you need more expertise in how to experience healing, take time today to find experts or books to make even more space for God to work in your life through the developed gifts and resources of others.

"For I will

pour water on

the thirsty land."

ISAIAH 44:3

Begin with Healing

2

In week three of *Rhythms*, we're looking at rhythms that make space for the daily healing we need.

The rigors of daily life, not even including the tougher seasons we all experience, seem to leave us battered and bruised in one way or another. Whether it's exhaustion, emotional hurts, or the physical effects of stress and anxiety, we desperately need to discover how to receive the healing our good God longs to give.

Today, we're looking at the opportunity to begin each day with healing, that we might venture every day out into the world restored and ready to partner with God to see his kingdom come.

May we find rhythms each day this week that prepare us, mind, body, and soul, to receive continual healing.

SCRIPTURE

"For I will pour water on the thirsty land, and streams on the dry ground." —Isaiah 44:3a

Devotional

As life has picked up the pace in the last eighteen months or so, I have honestly really struggled with my mornings. Every day, it's a difficult choice to give my focused attention to God when work, family, and personal needs are vying for my attention.

But I know, beyond any doubt, that the days I give myself to God first are measurably better than the days I don't. How I begin my day dictates the way the rest of my day will go. And that's because our first actions, our first decisions set our feet on a path that can sometimes be hard to return from.

If I begin with social media, scrolling through my feed to see what happened overnight, it's easy to spend the rest of my day struggling with comparison and consumption, being reactive to others instead of proactive in getting the most out of what God has for me.

If I begin with email or work, trying to get a head start on productivity for the day, it's easy to spend the rest of my day buying in to the notion that my highest value is doing rather than being, and seeking affirmation and joy in the production of results.

If I begin my day by meeting the needs of my family, I never seem to be able to serve them with true love and affection. I end up simply trying to get through the day with them rather than having the capacity and perspective to soak up all the love and goodness that exist in every moment with them.

But if I begin my day with God, experiencing the satisfaction and satiation that comes from simply resting in his presence, then and only then do I have a real chance to live my day fully on purpose, abiding in God and investing myself in what matters most.

One of the best reasons to begin the day with God is to make space to receive his healing and rejuvenation; we can experience his grace, forgiveness, and power right at the beginning of the day and go out into the rest of the day actually empowered to love him, ourselves, and others well.

Psalm 143:8 says, *"Let me hear in the morning of your steadfast love, for in you I trust. Make me know the way I should go, for to you I lift up my soul."* Lamentations 3:22–23 says, *"The steadfast love of the Lord never ceases; his mercies never come to an end; they are new every morning; great is your faithfulness."*

Imagine starting your day off healed, beginning work or time with family from a place of wholeness. So often the stresses and wounds from days add up, stacking on top of one another and weighing us down until we're burned out. But if God's mercies "are new every morning," we don't have to begin our days weighed down. Every day we can say "yes" to God's mercy and experience the healing we need in the morning.

Take time today to bring the stresses, burdens, or wounds that are weighing you down right now before the new mercy of your God. And experience what the rest of your day is like healed and renewed.

MEDITATION

Before conversing with God, take a few deep breaths, in and out, in and out, in and out. And slowly close your eyes and simply focus on being present in this moment.

Think about the last few mornings. Do you normally wake up with stress or peace? When you sense peace, what do you think is the source?

When you're stressed, what's the cause?

Imagine God shining a light on your mornings, giving you insight into the opportunity to begin every day with healing.

CONVERSATION

To help you gather your thoughts and write down what you sense God is saying, grab a journal if you can:

1. Write down what usually brings you stress in the mornings. Ask God for wisdom and insight into how to go through your morning with peace.

2. Write down what brings you peace in the morning. Ask God to bring thoughts and ideas to your mind of how you might better begin with healing.

3. Finally, take time to experience the peace and healing of God right now. Invite God's presence to the place of stress, pain, or worry. Lay your burdens down at the feet of God.

When you begin your day with healing, the impact will not only benefit you, but it'll benefit everyone you come into contact with today. When we begin with healing, we tap into what we need to offer our best to a world that's in desperate need.

What God does in your life doesn't end with you—it always works through you for another.

 My growth tracker   S M T W T F S

ACTION

Before you go to sleep tonight, remind yourself to begin your day with healing tomorrow. Don't judge yourself if you feel stressed or burdened. It's impossible to avoid the stresses of this life.

But don't stay there when God is inviting you to the place of healing and restoration.

"HEAL ME, O LORD."

PSALM 6:2

End with Healing

In week three of *Rhythms*, we're looking at rhythms that make space for the daily healing we need.

Simply the rigors of daily life, not even including the tougher seasons we all experience, seem to leave us battered and bruised in one way or another. Whether it's exhaustion, emotional hurts, or the physical effects of stress and anxiety, we desperately need to discover how to receive the healing our good God longs to give.

Yesterday, we looked at the opportunity to begin each day with healing, that we might venture every day out into the world restored and ready to partner with God to see his kingdom come. Today, we're going to explore how we can end our day with healing, and the power that comes from fostering moments of healing with God as bookends to our days.

May we find rhythms each day this week that prepare us, mind, body, and soul, to receive continual healing.

SCRIPTURE

"**Be gracious to me, O Lord, for I am languishing; heal me, O Lord, for my bones are troubled.**" —Psalm 6:2

Devotional

The way we begin and end our day often frames in our minds and hearts the experiences, both good and bad, that happen in between. As bookends contain within them stories, struggles, and ideas, so our rhythms for morning and night hold together the stories, struggles, and ideas of our day.

Yesterday, we explored the idea of beginning our day with healing, allowing God to rejuvenate and restore us so that we might venture out into our day from a place of wholeness. I truly believe there is no greater decision we can make to live our days with purpose and passion than to begin them with God.

But there is an often forgotten rhythm, those last moments of the day before we fall asleep, that also contain exponential power in our lives. If you look back at the last five nights, what was the last thing you did before you fell asleep? How do you normally spend those last moments of the day?

If I'm honest, at night I tend to try to squeeze in one more show, get a few more scrolls through my social feed, or even clear my inbox and check my calendar to get a jump start on the next day. And when I look at the effects of those actions, I realize that none of them position me to get the best night sleep I can, and none of them help me process and heal from the inevitable challenges and even wounds I experienced during the day.

There is a powerful, historical Christian practice I've been trying to implement into my rhythm that has been used by Christians for millennia to end their days well. It's called the examen. St. Ignatius of Loyola in his *Spiritual Exercises* provides a wealth of resources to deepen our understanding and experience of God. But perhaps my favorite exercise is the examen.

In its simplest form, the examen follows these five steps:

1. Become aware of God's presence.
2. Review the day with gratitude.
3. Pay attention to your emotions.
4. Choose one feature of the day and pray from it (e.g., an interaction with a friend or a moment of gratitude).
5. Look toward tomorrow.

In speaking about the importance of transforming our pain, Richard Rohr offers these important words:

> If we do not transform our pain, we will most assuredly transmit it— usually to those closest to us: our family, our neighbors, our coworkers, and, invariably, the most vulnerable, our children.[5]

I know that the stresses of my life, the wounds I experience either in actuality or through assumption, continually affect me and prohibit my ability to be a joyful and loving leader, spouse, and father. Imagine if we spent even ten minutes at the end of our days offering God the opportunity to transform our pain that we might not transmit it into the next day.

How would making space for God to provide perspective and healing over the hardships you face on a daily basis change your experience every day? How valuable would a ten-minute nightly examen be to your life?

Every evening, God is available to you with his loving presence, ready to speak kind wisdom and bring healing over your day. The opportunity, the invitation extended to you and me, is to simply say yes to him in the last moments of our day. If we will awaken to an awareness of God's presence and reawaken that awareness in the quiet of the night, I believe we will experience a transformation and empowerment we didn't know was possible.

So as we move to a time of meditation and conversation, I want to encourage you to practice the examen. Begin in meditation with an awareness of God's presence, review today or the day before, and pay attention to the emotions you feel.

Then as we move to a time of conversation, choose intentionally to bring your awareness, review, and emotions to God that he might speak directly into your life.

 MEDITATION

As we begin, take a few moments to set aside any distraction and simply be present with God and yourself right now. Take a few deep breaths and close your eyes.

Now, think about the things that tend to weigh you down in the evening. Maybe it's preemptively feeling the pressures of tomorrow. Maybe it's replaying the stressful events of the day.

Sit for a second, imagining a normal evening for you. Allow the Spirit to shine his light, that he might guide you to a new normal.

 CONVERSATION

To help you process your thoughts and understand better what God is speaking, grab a journal as we begin a time of conversation:

1. Write down some common experiences you have in the evening. How do the wounds and burdens of the day affect you?

2. Now read Matthew 6:34 and write down what you sense the Spirit is revealing to you through his word.

    "Therefore do not be anxious about tomorrow, for tomorrow will be anxious for itself." —Matthew 6:34

3. What's a simple rhythm you could use to end your day with healing? How could you quickly find restoration every night so that the burdens and the cares of the day don't pile on one another, day after day?

Often, we wait far too long before we bring our wounds before God.

And the little marks left on us after every day can add up to despair, discontent, and discouragement.

But why wait to experience healing when God is with you in every moment? Why allow the cares and burdens of this life to weigh you down any longer than they have to?

My growth tracker   S M T W T F S

ACTION

Set an alarm for ten minutes before you intend to fall asleep tonight. Place a journal and pen on your nightstand or bed. Choose tonight to set down or turn off a screen, and spend your last moments in the healing presence of God.

If you're looking for a greater understanding of the examen, as well as other spiritual exercises that can help you forge a greater awareness of God and yourself, a great resource is *Spiritual Exercises* by St. Ignatius of Loyola.

[5] Richard Rohr, *A Spring Within Us: A Book of Daily Meditations* (CAC Publishing: 2016), pg. 199, 120–121.

"Draw near to God,

and he will

draw near to you."

JAMES 4:8

Invitation

DAY

4

In week three of *Rhythms*, we're looking at rhythms that make space for the daily healing we need.

The rigors of daily life, not even including the tougher seasons we all experience, seem to leave us battered and bruised in one way or another. Whether it's exhaustion, emotional hurts, or the physical effects of stress and anxiety, we desperately need to discover how to receive the healing our good God longs to give.

Today, we're going to look at the invitation of God to receive the daily healing that we need, as well as how we can invite God to meet us in our places of weariness and wounding.

May we find rhythms each day this week that prepare us, mind, body, and soul, to receive continual healing.

SCRIPTURE

"Draw near to God, and he will draw near to you." —James 4:8

Devotional

One of the great realities of a relationship with God, a symptom of his love and grace, is that he never forces his desires or even good gifts on us. Life with God is about listening for his quiet invitation and saying "yes" as wholly and quickly as we can. And so it is with healing.

Every day, God makes his healing available to us. At the most foundational level, his salvation is available to all, yet is not forced upon us. A part of the mystery of faith is the need for us to say "yes" to even a gift like salvation. God's healing and covering for all our sins is as close as a "first, true yes" to him within our hearts.

But every day, there is healing God wants to provide for those wounds caused by this world we live in. But that healing is never forced upon us; rather, it's extended to us in the form of an invitation. And part of living an abundant life in God is developing rhythms to live in a constant state of "yes" to God's invitations, a posture of receiving we must embody in heart, body, and mind.

We must acknowledge that a "yes" to God's invitation is in fact at odds with the very structure and systems we're living in. Saying "yes" to God often requires slowing down, being still, and making space for God to work at a depth that's beyond words or understanding. When we move to action, we do so for his glory rather than for our own.

In Matthew 10:39, Jesus says, *"Whoever finds his life will lose it, and whoever loses his life for my sake will find it."* Somehow, abundant life in God comes not by looking for the easy path, the path of self-gain, but by denying ourselves, picking up our crosses, and following the ways and person of Jesus (Luke 9:23).

A "yes" to God is oftentimes a "no" to the world around us. When the world says that the morning is a time to get ahead on the day, Jesus says it's a time to root and ground ourselves in him. When the world says that financial security and abundance is a cornerstone of a happy life, Scripture teaches that "the love of money is a root of all kinds of evils" (1 Tim. 6:10). And when the world teaches us that rest and recovery is a sign and symptom of weakness, God modeled for us in the creation narrative and in his command for the Sabbath that rest is good, holy, and woven into the very fabric of our being, our faith, and our world.

So today, think for a moment about the rhythms of your life. Which rhythms are right now helping you say "yes" to God? Which rhythms for work and rest have a "yes" to God at their core, and which rhythms are saying "yes" to the world or your own wrongful desires?

Which rhythms could you keep or create to live with a deeper and more frequent "yes" to God? And what do you need to say "no" to today so that you might have space for more and better "yeses"?

If I may, here are a few rhythms that are helping me say "yes" to God, as well as a few "nos" that I need to voice often.

Rhythm One: Keep the Sabbath.

Genesis 2:2–3 tells us, *"And on the seventh day God finished his work that he had done, and he rested on the seventh day from all his work that he had done. So God blessed the seventh day and made it holy, because on it God rested from all his work that he had done in creation."*

God, a perfect being with no weakness, a being who dwells in all of eternity and does not need rest or sleep, chooses to rest as an act of holiness, goodness, and celebration.

Ezekiel 20:20 says, *"Keep my Sabbaths holy that they may be a sign between me and you, that you may know that I am the LORD your God."*

A weekly day of real rest from both career work and family work creates a rhythm that both helps us heal and recover, but also sets our feet on God's path instead of the world's.

Hear me say that taking a real Sabbath might not only require saying no to work in your career, school, or with your family, but it might require also even saying no to your church. It is entirely possible that our churches, especially in the way of busyness and emphasis on service and work, are conforming to the world rather than the call of God. When church vibrancy is measured by increased attendance, better services, bigger buildings, and financial revenue, and churchgoers funneled into a system that drives these goals, I worry that church is at times at odds with experiencing a true Sabbath rather than a catalyst to a day of rest.

So, my encouragement is simply this: set aside a day a week that is purely for enjoyment of God, enjoyment of family and friends, and connection and deep rest for yourself. If that needs to be a different day than Sunday, especially if you're a church leader or heavily involved in service at your church, make the space for it.

Rhythm Two: Spend your first moments alone with God.

With the very existence of First15, and how much I have been talking about the value of spending time alone with God, I will keep this brief! There is no more important daily practice in saying "yes" to God's invitation of healing than beginning your day in God's presence.

The "yes" of spending your most important moments of the day with God makes it worlds easier to live with an abiding "yes" throughout the rest of your day. And the alternative is equally true. It's truly challenging to say "yes" to God when we begin our day by saying "yes" to work, entertainment, social media, our appearance, exercise, family, or news.

Rhythm Three: Retreat.

Just as a weekly Sabbath provides a day of retreat, I believe there are two other rhythms of retreat and rest that empower us to accept God's invitation to healing.

If we can take a day a week, a day a month, and a few days a year to retreat from the world, be still, and rest in reading, worship, meditation, and conversation with God, those rhythms will provide a greater power to say "yes" to God and "no" to everything else than we can imagine.

Our need for rest, for solitude and silence, for pure and focused connection to God and ourselves is wired into our very being. Jesus needed to retreat (Matthew 4). He led his disciples to retreat (Mark 6:31). Throughout Christian history, our greatest leaders have practiced rhythms of retreating.

If right now your life consists of just work and vacation, and there is no rhythm in your life for a spiritual retreat, you have the opportunity to create and abide in a rhythm of rest and empowerment that God is right now inviting you into.

Take time in meditation and conversation to process the areas where you can say "yes" to God's invitation to healing and "no" to that which is at odds with God's invitation. Be honest with yourself and know that your life is actually in your control. You can make real changes to your life that connect you to God, yourself, and others. Your life can embody the power of God's healing that comes through rest and rejuvenation in the Spirit.

Make space now for God to show you how.

MEDITATION

Take time now to settle into a few moments of quiet.

Take a few deep breaths, place to the side any distractions or feelings of rush and hurry, and choose to be still with God.

Say "yes" to God's presence that is already with you and around you.

Reflect with him on where you can create rhythms for "yes," as well as things you can say "no" to in order to better receive God's healing and abundant life.

CONVERSATION

Grab a journal if you can to better process your thoughts, feelings, and God's responses:

1. Process your need for God's healing. What would a more frequent and deeper "yes" to God's healing produce in your life?

2. What do you need to say "no" to in order to say "yes" to God's invitation to healing more often?

3. What rhythms can you create to better empower yourself to say "yes" to God's healing? Choose action steps that are fully possible today rather than seeking to reorient your entire life, unless you feel the need to take drastic measures.

If your ability to implement rhythms for healing that you need will create changes in your interactions at work, with family, or at church, take time today to write out what you will need to say to others around you.

Creating boundaries is not always a fun process, and not always something even those who love us are comfortable with. But in boundaries and the formation of new rhythms, ultimately we will be better equipped and empowered to love and care for others.

My growth tracker S M T W T F S

ACTION

If you are in a place of healing today, where you feel refreshed and rejuvenated by God, take an opportunity today to join with God in extending his invitation of healing to others.

Proverbs 16:24 says, "Gracious words are like a honeycomb, sweetness to the soul and health to the body." One of the best ways you can partner with God in his work of healing is through your words. Speaking life, peace, and love over others in a way that requires vulnerability and openness on our part is a powerful way to soften the hearts of others to say "yes" to God.

Through your words today, join with God's work of healing and life, especially for those around you who might need a touch of his presence the most.

"Do not be anxious."

MATTHEW 6:34

Healing Moments

5

In week three of *Rhythms*, we're looking at rhythms that make space for the daily healing we need.

The rigors of daily life, not even including the tougher seasons we all experience, seem to leave us battered and bruised in one way or another. Whether it's exhaustion, emotional hurts, or the physiological effects of stress and anxiety, we desperately need to discover how to receive the healing our good God longs to give.

Today, we're going to focus on living in the moment, and how when we are fully present with God and ourselves, we naturally make space for God to move and work to the fullest.

May we find rhythms each day this week that prepare us, mind, body, and soul, to receive continual healing.

"Therefore do not be anxious about tomorrow, for tomorrow will be anxious for itself. Sufficient for the day is its own trouble." —Matthew 6:34

Devotional

You and I are beings that can only be in the present. While our Creator dwells in all of eternity, we only have the moment we're living in right now.

But we spend so much of our energy planning for or even worrying over the future and dwelling on the past. And to be sure, there is a place for planning, as well as learning, from the past. Both can be critical in making the most of our present. But the problem sets in when we allow our minds and our hearts to be drawn so deeply into either the past or present that we fail to even notice, let alone experience, what God is doing in and around us right now. In Matthew 6:25–29, Jesus speaks these beautiful words over us:

> *Therefore I tell you, do not be anxious about your life, what you will eat or what you will drink, nor about your body, what you will put on. Is not life more than food, and the body more than clothing? Look at the birds of the air: they neither sow nor reap nor gather into barns, and yet your heavenly Father feeds them. Are you not of more value than they? And which of you by being anxious can add a single hour to his span of life? And why are you anxious*

about clothing? Consider the lilies of the field, how they grow: they neither toil nor spin, yet I tell you, even Solomon in all his glory was not arrayed like one of these.

All of creation models for us the beauty of being in the present. The birds of the air, the lilies of the field simply seek to fulfill the purpose for which they were created in this moment, not trying to become something more, and not settling for something less.

To be present, to lay down the unhealthy parts of dwelling on the past and planning for the future, is an act of trust. It is a posture that declares that God alone is God, he alone holds eternity in the palm of his hand, and he alone guides and directs our steps on the path he has laid before us. In the same way, being present is a posture that declares to ourselves that we are not God, we do not have control over the future, and we in and of ourselves cannot find true healing from our past.

And most importantly, being present positions us to invite God to meet us fully where we are, being aware of and opening up those hidden places in our hearts and those seemingly subconscious patterns of thought that can have such a negative impact on our life.

When we are fully present with ourselves and God, we create the best possible space for God to bring healing. It's when we are present with our pain, when we see and comprehend its underlying sources, that we invite God to do his healing work. It's when we are present with our fears, acknowledging those places where we are grasping for control that we can never attain, that we allow God to bring us to a place of peace birthed from trust. It's when we are present with the lies we are believing that we make room for the Holy Spirit to pluck out the flaming darts fired by the evil one that are twisting our understanding of ourselves, our God, and the world around us.

In reality, choosing to be present is entirely countercultural. Our world seems to offer us limitless ways to distract ourselves from the present. There is more entertainment being created and streamed on more devices than we can use at any given moment than we could ever hope to consume. Social media is literally created to pull us in and keep us immersed, giving us the hope of a reward of laughter, anger, or knowledge just always another swipe away.

But as we seek to be connected with the world around us, I fear we are losing connecting with ourselves. As we seek to know and be known through these sources of digital connection, I fear we know and allow ourselves to be known by God less and less.

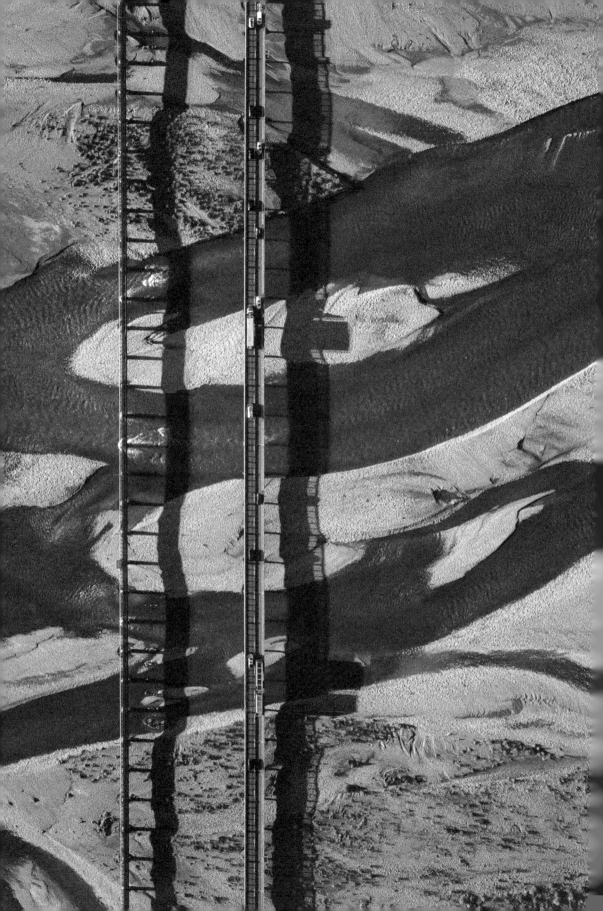

We are losing that which is most important, that which is most core as we're pulled away by that which is merely brightest and loudest.

What we need are rhythms that help us be present with ourselves, with God, and with others again. What we need is to create spaces where we set aside that which is superfluous for that which is most important. What we need is to choose a new way, which is really the ancient way, of peace and trust and relationship. And luckily, we have a helper in the Holy Spirit and stories of Christian practices to serve as a guide to a new, better normal.

So by way of rhythms, I want to first unpack tools we're giving you here to be present to God's healing moments in First15. And then explore a few rhythms and tools you can implement on your own as the best help for you to enjoy God and life.

Rhythm One: Be still with God.

As much as the word *meditation* is taboo currently among believers, we must acknowledge that meditation is both a biblical and important historical practice for us. Christians have turned to stillness and quiet since the birth of our faith to step outside of the rush and hurry and make space to experience God in the deepest way.

Every day with First15, we will give you space to reflect on those principles or ideas that most resonate with you, to be still and know that he is God (Ps. 46:10). The more space you are willing to make in meditation, the more time you are willing to be still and quiet, the more you will build a basis for being present and receiving God's healing moment to moment.

Rhythm Two: Apply scripture to your life.

Lectio Divina is a beautiful way of reading Scripture that invites the word of God to move from our heads to our hearts. It's a way of inviting the Holy Spirit to breathe life into the words he's inspired, that they might be illuminated and applied directly to our lives. It allows us to be more fully present with God's truth and makes space for God to correct lies and bring healing to our ways of thinking.

Rhythm Three: Confess and receive forgiveness.

We live with the guilt and shame of sin for far too long. While God has already forgiven every sin we will ever commit, all the weight of God's wrath poured out on Jesus on the cross, we still need to receive the power of God's forgiveness when we act against our new nature in him.

Confession creates moments of healing, where God can bring his love and grace into moments of mistakes, showing us just how unconditional his love truly is.

I'm not sure that there is anything more healing than seeing afresh how deeply God enjoys us even in the midst of our wrongs.

So as we move to a time of meditation and conversation, I want to encourage you right now to set aside every burden and distraction, and be as fully present with yourself and God as possible right now.

Believe that God has healing for you in this moment as you are present with him and as you open your hands and heart to receive his word.

 MEDITATION

Take a moment to pause and be as present in this moment as you can be. If your mind wanders, don't jolt it back. Peacefully redirect your attention to this moment whenever you think of the next.

Open your ears and take in the sounds happening around you at this moment. Be still with them.

Fill your lungs, slowly breathing in and out. Be present with the air moving in and out of you.

As you find a sense of stillness in this moment, begin a conversation with God.

 CONVERSATION

To help you process your thoughts and understand better what God is speaking, grab a journal as we begin a time of conversation:

1. What tends to draw your mind away from the moment? Is it memories from the past? Is it an imagination for the future? Write down what's common for your experience.

2. What do you notice happens to you when you're present and in the moment? What do you feel? What sort of effect are you left with? Write down your experiences.

3. What's a practical step you could take today to practice being more present, that you might experience healing in the moment? Take time to write down some options and pay attention to what resonates most with you.

The goal in being present isn't perfection, but practice. Given the stimulation and inundation of the days we're living in, it's harder but more beneficial than ever to focus on this moment.

But as believers, we're given the unique opportunity to hand our future over to a God we know to be real, to be loving, and to dwell in all of eternity. The question then becomes: how often are we willing to live differently and tap into the great opportunity of every moment?

 My growth tracker   S M T W T F S

ACTION

Take a few more moments today to practice being present that you might receive God's healing. Maybe set your timer for one minute and bring your entire focus into the moment you're in.

While God dwells in all of eternity, you only have this present moment. Choose to make the most of them today.

"WILL YOU BE TO ME

LIKE A DECEITFUL

BROOK, LIKE WATERS

THAT FAIL?"

JEREMIAH 15:18

Pain

DAY

6

In week three of *Rhythms*, we're looking at rhythms that make space for the daily healing we need.

The rigors of daily life, not even including the tougher seasons we all experience, seem to leave us battered and bruised in one way or another. Whether it's exhaustion, emotional hurts, or the physical effects of stress and anxiety, we desperately need to discover how to receive the healing our good God longs to give.

Today, we're going to look at the subject of pain, and how God in his kindness wants to guide our gaze to both see the truth about our wounds and bring us to a place of healing.

May we find rhythms each day this week that prepare us, mind, body, and soul, to receive continual healing.

SCRIPTURE

"Why is my pain unceasing, my wound incurable, refusing to be healed? Will you be to me like a deceitful brook, like waters that fail?" —Jeremiah 15:18

Devotional

One of the most basic realities of humanity that I fear our modern-day expression of Christianity acknowledges the least is pain and suffering. From the songs we sing on Sunday, to our stock answers to the question "How are you doing?" by and large we seem deeply uncomfortable with the reality of both our pain and the pain of others around us.

We move so quickly to problem-solving that I fear we blow past the first phase of healing, which is seeing and validating the pain, looking for the underlying causes, as well as its effects on us and others, and being patient with God as he does a deeper work than often our timetables allow for.

We love, myself included, the passages that promise healing, renewal, and joy. We will ourselves to endure hardships with hope and faith. And while all of that is good, right, and necessary, it's not the whole of the gift of healing available to us in God.

Sometimes the part of God's gift of healing we need the most is that he is well acquainted with grief (Isaiah 53:3); he was a man of many sorrows (Isaiah 53:3), and the God who weeps over the loss of a loved one (John 11:35).

Sometimes the gift we need is that God doesn't brush past the reality of our pain, even if it's uncomfortable. He sees it for what it is, mourns over it, and longs to provide at times simply the comfort of his presence in the midst of pain.

Jeremiah says in Jeremiah 15:18, *"Why is my pain unceasing, my wound incurable, refusing to be healed? Will you be to me like a deceitful brook, like waters that fail?"* David cries out in Psalm 22:1 the words Jesus himself would echo on the cross: *"My God, my God, why have you forsaken me? Why are you so far from saving me, from the words of my groaning?"*

One of the hardest experiences my wife and I have had to go through was a miscarriage. We genuinely felt that God had led us separately in prayer to begin trying for a child, and when we learned we were pregnant, we rejoiced and prepared for months. After the miscarriage, I struggled for weeks to approach God again. I had no grid for inviting God into my pain.

I asked God for an explanation and got nothing. I searched for understanding but couldn't rationalize our experience. Finally, I picked up my guitar and simply began to sing, expressing my anger, resentment, and pain. And in the first few moments, I felt God draw near to me, as he had numerous times before.

I didn't walk away from that experience with answers. I still don't understand. But I did walk away having met with God, allowing him into my pain, and learning that he is good even in the midst of it.

So, as we move into a time of meditation and conversation, I want you to approach God with whatever is causing you pain today. Maybe it's a hurtful phrase spoken from someone you trust. Maybe it's a physical pain you can't seem to get rid of. Maybe it's a broken trust between you and God.

Whatever pain comes to the surface today, rather than seeking the end of the pain, allow God to simply provide to you the gift of healing in the form of his nearness. Experience your grief, your sorrow, your pain together today. Entrust him as the guide to your healing both with the process and timing. And simply rest in his love.

MEDITATION

Begin by taking some time to feel what's happening in your heart, mind, and body.

Do you feel emotional pain resonating anywhere specifically? Don't judge how you feel—simply notice it. And allow yourself to sit with the reality of what you're experiencing right now.

Take a few moments to be still before conversing with God.

CONVERSATION

Grab a journal if you can to better process your thoughts, feelings, and God's responses:

1. Write down how you normally respond to pain. Do you seek to disassociate? Do you seek distraction? How do you normally deal with the reality of experiencing pain?

2. What would you imagine is the healthiest response you could have to pain? How would you imagine God is inviting you into the place of healing?

3. Take time to bring one area of pain before God right now and sit with his presence. Listen for anything he would speak. Notice any picture that comes to mind. Allow God to move and work any way he desires.

I'm often surprised how God invites me to the place of healing. Sometimes I just need stillness. Sometimes I need confession. Sometimes I need the truth. Sometimes I need the courage to seek healing from another.

Whatever path God has for us, I find it almost always starts best in the stillness of his presence.

ACTION

If you notice the area of pain coming back to mind, remind yourself of the healing moment you've had with God. Does your intuition tell you that there's more work to be done, or that you simply need to surrender?

Continue inviting God to the place of healing for whatever it is he highlighted in your life today. As you intentionally pursue healing, you'll discover a newfound freedom.

"Go in peace."

_____

MARK 5:34

Believe

7

In week three of Rhythms, we're looking at rhythms that make space for the daily healing we need.

The rigors of daily life, not even including the tougher seasons we all experience, seem to leave us battered and bruised in one way or another. Whether it's exhaustion, emotional hurts, or the physiological effects of stress and anxiety, we desperately need to discover how to receive the healing our good God longs to give.

But our God never forces even his best gifts upon us. He gently and purposefully invites us to receive them, to experience the abundant life he so desperately longs to give us. And healing is no different. To experience God's healing power even in the smallest of wounds, we need to believe that he is real, good, loving, and present with us in our pain.

May we find rhythms each day this week that prepare us, mind, body, and soul, to receive continual healing. And today, may we begin to believe that God is as good as he says he is.

SCRIPTURE

"'Daughter, your faith has made you well; go in peace, and be healed of your disease.'"
—Mark 5:34

Devotional

In Mark 5, we find a story of desperate faith and healing, a wounded woman pushing through the challenges in her way to touch God himself, and experience the power and presence she so desperately needed. Read this story this morning with open eyes and an open heart and allow God to speak to you through it:

> *And there was a woman who had had a discharge of blood for twelve years, and who had suffered much under many physicians, and had spent all that she had, and was no better but rather grew worse. She had heard the reports about Jesus and came up behind him in the crowd and touched his garment. For she said, "If I touch even his garments, I will be made well." And immediately the flow of blood dried up, and she felt in her body that she was healed of her disease. And Jesus, perceiving in himself that power had gone out from him, immediately turned about in the crowd and said, "Who touched my garments?" The woman, knowing what had happened to her, came in fear and trembling and fell down before him and told him the whole truth. And he said to her, "Daughter, your faith has made you well; go in peace, and be healed of your disease." —Mark 5:25–30, 33–34*

I don't pretend to understand the finer points of healing theology as it pertains to this story. The voice of Jesus declaring to this woman *"Your faith has made you well"* doesn't fit into the boxes of my understanding. But if you read through the Scriptures, you cannot mistake a connection between faith and receiving the gifts of God.

What I do know is: God never forces even his best gifts upon us. Salvation requires a "yes" in our heart to the reality of and relationship with God. Bearing eternal fruit requires a choice to abide in God, to yoke ourselves to him and stop going our own way. Peace requires a choice to trust God with our circumstances and lean into his goodness in the midst of challenges we don't understand.

And healing requires belief, an act of faith that makes space for God to see and touch the most vulnerable parts of us, believing that he is both willing and able to restore that which was broken.

Why God doesn't heal every time, I do not understand. Why there is so much brokenness when God is so good and so powerful does not make sense to me. But to avoid bringing our wounds to God, to avoid seeking his gift of healing for ourselves and others is to ignore the Scriptures and the stories of transformation happening all around us.

As we close this week on healing, seeking to develop rhythms that empower us to receive this vital gift of God moment by moment, there are a few rhythms to stir up belief I want to recommend today.

Rhythm One: Reflect on the Scriptures.

We need the Bible's compilation of stories to stir up our belief. We need to constantly remind ourselves how God has moved in power and love throughout the generations to stir up belief, especially in the hard times. Every day, we give you a chance to engage with the Scriptures in First15. Don't move past them quickly. Allow God's word to sink from your head to your heart through the practice of time, stillness, and reflection.

Rhythm Two: Pray for belief.

My prayers in hard times often echo that of the Father in Mark 9:24, saying, *"I believe; help my unbelief!"*

A rise of belief begins not by faking our way to faith, but by acknowledging our lack of it. It's only in truth and authenticity that God can meet us fully where we are and take us somewhere better. If you lack belief, see it fully and lay it before the feet of Jesus, and in the midst of his presence, allow him to give you a greater measure of faith.

Rhythm Three: Choose faith.

At the end of the day, there will always be a reason to doubt. A faith built on 100 percent assurance is not possible. And anyone who is, or proclaims to be without doubt in some form, is blinding themselves to the mystery of God and the bigger picture of life.

Faith is not the absence of doubt, but rather a choice to believe in the midst of it.

So when you are facing a Y in the road, the path to healing is choosing to believe in the face of uncertainty. It's in the choice of faith that we posture ourselves to receive whatever gift God wants to give. It's in saying "yes" to God even when we have reasons to say "no" that position ourselves under the reality that his ways are higher than ours. His greater story is better and more beautiful than one we could craft on our own.

So today, as we move to a time of meditation and conversation, may God show us where we lack faith. May we have the courage to bring our doubts before God openly and honestly. May we choose to lay them at the feet of Jesus, not ignoring them, but allowing him to move in power and understanding in the midst of them.

May we experience the healing we need as we simply say "yes" to God, touching his robe in faith and desperation today. And may we walk away from God's presence hearing the voice of Jesus proclaim over us, *"Your faith has made you well."*

 MEDITATION

Take some time to stir up your faith today.

Reflect on the goodness of God. Sit with the reality of it.

Reflect on things he's done in your life. Be thankful.

And take some deep breaths as you draw your focus to the goodness of this moment.

To help you process your thoughts and understand better what God is speaking, grab a journal as we begin a time of conversation:

1. Write down any thoughts that were prevalent in your mind as you were reading the devotional today. Acknowledge any questions you have about faith and accept that they are good.

2. Write down what changes in your heart and mind as you focus on faith. What stresses fall away? What courage do you begin to sense? How do you imagine stirring up faith and belief could affect your day-to-day life?

3. What's happening in your life that you need faith for today? Take a moment and invite God to illuminate a path to greater faith and belief.

Faith doesn't obligate God to move. I find that faith simply positions us to receive what God already wants to give. He's not a God who forces even the best things on us. We have to say "yes" to what's from him and "no" to what's not.

Keep your faith today and find the peace and purpose that come from being better positioned to receive whatever it is that God longs to give.

My growth tracker   S M T W T F S

ACTION

Notice, without judgment or shame, when you feel doubt today. Rather than ignoring it, take some time to bring it before God.

In this life, there will be questions left unanswered. Christianity is not a religion of right answers, but an invitation to a life-giving relationship.

Grow in your comfort with questions today, but in tandem, take time to stir up your faith.

WEEK FOUR

wisdom

"If any of you lacks
wisdom, let him ask God."

JAMES 1:5

Wisdom from God

1

In the Scriptures, we find the story of Solomon, a king blessed with wealth beyond measure, because rather than asking for wealth or status, he simply asked for wisdom.

And as he gained wisdom from God, that wisdom brought life and abundance.

In week four of *Rhythms*, we're exploring how we can make room moment by moment to receive the wisdom from God we so desperately need. We all have questions that need answers. None of us knows the best way forward at any given moment.

But thankfully, we are the children of a God who gives wisdom beyond measure. May we learn to open our hands, minds, and hearts this week to receive the wisdom of our all-loving, all-knowing God.

SCRIPTURE

"If any of you lacks wisdom, let him ask God, who gives generously to all without reproach, and it will be given him." —James 1:5

Devotional

I wonder how many missed opportunities I've had to allow God to move in greater ways in and around me. Every day, God provides more healing than I make space to receive. Every day, God is speaking, but I am too busy or distracted to listen. And every day, God has wisdom he desires to give generously, but I fail to simply ask him for it.

But today is a new day. Today is a fresh chance to lean not into my own wisdom, the lessons I've learned in my limited time on this earth, but to ask for and receive the wisdom of the ages—insights from the Creator, Seer, and Sustainer of all.

James 1:5, our verse for today, says, *"If any of you lacks wisdom, let him ask God, who gives generously to all without reproach, and it will be given him."* The Scriptures promise not only that God will give us wisdom if we ask for it, but that he will give it *"generously"* and *"without reproach."*

For God to be without reproach in offering wisdom means he does not disapprove of your lack of knowledge or insight. He is not disappointed with your need for insight and help. God has seen every day of our life. He knows the fragility of our frame, the limit of our capacities. Psalm 103:14 says, *"He remembers that we are dust."*

If we will humble ourselves, even just for a moment, I think we'll find beauty in the sentiment of the Scriptures. God did not create you and me to be self-sufficient, no matter what our society says. He does not expect us to have everything together, to have all the intuition, all the insight, all the knowledge we need to be successful in life on our own.

Instead, he created you and me for relationship. To be self-sufficient is to decide that relationships are a luxury, not a necessity. To have all the wisdom we need is to declare ourselves to be Lord of our own lives, the Shepherd instead of a sheep.

Scripture is clear that to receive God's wisdom, we have to ask for it. But why is it that asking for help can be so challenging? Why is it that we can have access to all wisdom in the Holy Spirit, in the Scriptures, in wise counselors around us, but we choose instead to go our own way?

I know in my life, it seems that my pride and the values of my society work together in an attempt to keep me isolated, to prove my worth on my own, to make something of myself. I desperately need a daily reminder, first thing, that God's ways are higher, that his ways are better. That he says I am valuable before I've done a thing of merit or worth.

This week, we're looking at rhythms to seek and find the wisdom of God. But the place to begin those rhythms is simple yet incredibly difficult. It's a place of humility, a posture of weakness, an acknowledgment of insufficiency. But as all postures of humility are, it's the only true place of power.

So, as we begin this exciting week, lowering ourselves into the endless well of God's wisdom, I have one rhythm to offer you today.

As you do First15, or use whatever tool or framework you have for meeting with God, take time in meditation and conversation to humble yourself before God.

Practically, I seek to humble myself in a few ways.

First, take a physical posture of humility. Intentionally bow your head as you would to a king. Open your hands in prayer as a sign that your heart, your mind, and your life are open to God.

Second, acknowledge your weakness to God. Use your words to proclaim to yourself and to your Father that he alone is God, and you are not.

Last, thank God that he does not come to you with reproach, that he is not disappointed with your lack, but rather thrilled for your desire for a relationship. And allow thankfulness to bring you closer to the loving heart of God.

As we move to a time of meditation and conversation, reflect on the power of humility as it positions you to find the strength and wisdom of God.

MEDITATION

As we begin, bow your head with intention. Open your hands as a declaration. Breathe deeply a few times, in and out, in and out, in and out.

And in a posture of humility, simply lift your heart to God. Find that place of connection between your spirit and the Holy Spirit, and rest.

CONVERSATION

And now as we move to a time of conversation, grab a journal if you can to aid in your ability to ask for and receive the wisdom of God:

1. Begin by journaling or verbalizing your weakness to God. This is not a time to beat yourself down, or to practice false humility. Look for ways that your capacities simply are not the same as God's and choose to see clearly your need for God's wisdom.

2. And next, where do you need wisdom most today? What area of your life—whether it be a relationship, a decision, an emotion, a wound—do you need God's wisdom the most? Process that area with God.

3. Now ask God for his wisdom and pay attention to any thoughts, Scriptures, pictures, or emotions that rise up in you. Process what you believe God to be saying, ask more questions about it, and don't move out of the time of conversation until you have the clarity you need.

Part of receiving God's wisdom is being willing to trust in his ability to speak to you. Hearing God's voice is something that requires faith and practice. And typically, it's in choosing to take action on what you believe

God spoke that leads to greater levels of confidence in hearing God, and more consistency in asking him for wisdom.

So, as we look for a step of action to take today, choose faith instead of doubt that God is good enough to speak a word of wisdom to you today.

ACTION

As you go out into the rest of your day today, choose to ask God for his wisdom when you're not sure which way to go. When you come to a crossroads or up against a challenge, take just a moment to reconnect your spirit with God's Spirit and ask for wisdom.

Then commit to following that wisdom in faith, knowing that it is truly okay to make a mistake.

May God lead you to a posture of humility today and instill in you the practice of seeking and finding his generous wisdom as we make space every day this week to grow together.

"BLESSED IS THE ONE

WHO FINDS WISDOM."

PROVERBS 3:13

Ask and Receive

DAY

2

In the Scriptures, we find the story of Solomon, a king blessed with wealth beyond measure because rather than asking for wealth or status, he simply asked for wisdom.

And as he gained wisdom from God, that wisdom brought life and abundance.

In week four of *Rhythms*, we're exploring how we can make room moment by moment to receive the wisdom from God we so desperately need. We all have questions that need answers. None of us knows the best way forward at any given moment.

And today, we're going to look specifically at how we conceptually and practically ask for and receive wisdom.

May we learn to open our hands, minds, and hearts this week to receive the wisdom of our all-loving, all-knowing God.

SCRIPTURE

"Blessed is the one who finds wisdom, and the one who gets understanding, for the gain from her is better than gain from silver and her profit better than gold." —Proverbs 3:13–14

Devotional

Too often, I find it sincerely challenging to ask for help. Part of me loves the satisfaction of having figured it out on my own. Part of me worries what others will think of me if I don't know something I probably should know.

There's a stereotype about men you'll see often depicted in stories. The family is lost. The dad is driving. And rather than asking for directions to the destination, he claims that he really does know where he's going and is just taking a scenic route.

But beyond stereotypical actions of dads, I think we all want to know what to do. Lately, when I ask my toddler if he knows something, he always says "yes." But then he looks at me, waiting for me to explain it. I remember stories my parents would tell of my youth when my brother and I would shirk their help with the phrase "my byself."

There is something in our human condition that makes it hard to ask for help. It's there when we're little. It's there when we're in school. It's there when we venture out on our own. And it shows right back up if we have the chance to have kids of our own.

But there is an abundance of Scriptures proving the reality that we are at our strongest not through our own capacities, but when we ask for and receive the strength of God.

2 Corinthians 12:9–11 says:

> *But he said to me, "My grace is sufficient for you, for my power is made perfect in weakness." Therefore I will boast all the more gladly about my weaknesses, so that Christ's power may rest on me. For the sake of Christ, then, I am content with weaknesses, insults, hardships, persecutions, and calamities. For when I am weak, then I am strong.*

2 Timothy 4:17a says, *"But the Lord stood by me and strengthened me."* In reference to prayer, Romans 8:26a says, *"Likewise the Spirit helps us in our weakness."* Isaiah 40:31 doesn't say that those who run ahead will find strength, but that *"they who wait for the Lord shall renew their strength."* And Jesus says in Matthew 16:25, *"Whoever loses his life for my sake will find it."*

In this weeklong focus on wisdom, the simple rhythms we need to adopt build on yesterday's focus on humility. To find wisdom, we have to first ask for it, and then learn how to receive it. As simple as it may sound, both asking and receiving are at odds with our world's way of living. Asking and receiving in their very actions require humility and a realization that true strength doesn't come from within ourselves, but in God alone.

God has amazing promises for you and me today as we choose to seek his wisdom. James 1:5 says, *"If any of you lacks wisdom, let him ask God, who gives generously to all without reproach, and it will be given him."* And the wisdom God gives isn't harsh or conceited. But instead, James 3:17 says, *"But the wisdom from above is first pure, then peaceable, gentle, open to reason, full of mercy and good fruits, impartial and sincere."*

So first, how do we ask for wisdom?

We begin by first adopting a posture of vulnerability and openness, laying down anything we are holding too tightly and making space for God to speak. It does no good to ask if we don't want to receive.

Then we must ask with faith that God does and will speak. We have to lean on the Scriptures that declare that God not only gives wisdom, but he gives it *"generously"* (James 1:5).

Ask God with faith and belief that as much as you desire wisdom, he desires it for you even more. As much as you want to know his will, he desires to lead and guide you down the narrow path to an abundant life even more as your Good Shepherd.

So, ask with faith and vulnerability, allowing God to speak directly to those areas you need wisdom in the most. Lean on the Holy Spirit. Give up the expectation of doing life on your own. And lead into the immense opportunity that comes with being a child of God, a sheep not a shepherd, of being a part of the body instead of the head.

And next, once we've asked for wisdom, how do we receive it?

Really, this question could be said differently: "How do I hear the voice of God?" It's a question I've asked and get asked often. It's a practice that requires faith, demands failure, and produces as much life as other spiritual disciplines that Christians often emphasize.

What is both wonderful and challenging about receiving wisdom and direction from God is that God has the ability to speak in ways far more vast and far deeper than you and I have. He's able to use literally every sense we have, able to use others, able to use situations and Scripture and the wisdom of books both faith-centric and not. His voice echoes through every facet of life if we will simply have the ears to hear it.

The act of receiving wisdom from God is done best when we allow him to speak how he sees fit, rather than how we wish he would. For those who look only to open doors to walk through as God's wisdom, you are missing his desire to speak through your intuition, through research, directly from his voice to your spirit, and untold other ways he wants to guide you.

For those who look only to intuition, you are missing the opportunity to glean wisdom from wise counsel, from the Scriptures, from situations, from logic and reason.

For those who simply do as their mentors, parents, and pastors say, you are missing the reality that God speaks to you first and foremost. Wise counsel is best taken when it resonates with what God has already been speaking to you, but you didn't have the language or faith to act on it yet.

So said simply, to receive the wisdom from God is to listen with every fiber of our being until we have a sense enough to act on, knowing that we will inevitably get something wrong. And to fail is to be human. And God does not expect anything more from us than who we are in this moment. He remembers our frame. He knows our limitations. And he loves us unconditionally anyway.

So today, as we move to a time of meditation and conversation, make space to ask God for and receive the wisdom of God. May you hear his voice in deeper and more profound ways today. And may you discover the strength that comes in the midst of weakness and learn to live according to the upside principles of God's kingdom, because there is truly no better way to live.

Take some time to reflect on the goodness and wisdom of God.

Begin by taking a few breaths, in and out, slowly. Meditate on the goodness and wisdom of God who is within you.

Think about the great opportunity of your Creator and Sustainer dwelling within you, longing to guide you to wisdom.

CONVERSATION

Now, as we move to a time of conversation, grab a journal if you can to aid in your ability to ask for and receive the wisdom of God.

1. Write down where you need the most wisdom today. Maybe it's a pathway forward. Maybe it's an unanswered question. Clarify the question you most want wisdom from God on.

2. Ask God for wisdom and wait with peace and expectation for him to answer in any way he desires.

3. Write down as clearly as you can the sense you have from God. What is wisdom on the subject? What can you do practically to implement wisdom into this area of your life?

Walking in wisdom is saying "yes" to the tension of humility and confidence. We will absolutely get things wrong when we try to seek after God. But the only way to instill his wisdom as deeply as possible is to move forward with the sense we have with confidence.

Don't fear being wrong. There is grace upon grace as you do your best.

 My growth tracker   S M T W T F S

ACTION

Whenever you come upon a question, take a second and invite the wisdom of God into your circumstance. If you don't sense anything, don't worry about it! But it never hurts to ask God if he desires to speak into a scenario you're not sure about.

"Get wisdom, and whatever

you get, get insight."

PROVERBS 4:7

Rhythms of Wisdom

DAY

3

In the Scriptures, we find the story of Solomon, a king blessed with wealth beyond measure because rather than asking for wealth or status, he simply asked for wisdom.

And as he gained wisdom from God, that wisdom brought life and abundance.

In week four of *Rhythms*, we're exploring how we can make room moment by moment to receive the wisdom from God we so desperately need. We all have questions that need answers. None of us knows the best way forward at any given moment.

And today, we're focusing specifically on the rhythms of life that create opportunities for us to gain the wisdom of God more deeply and more consistently.

May we learn to open our hands, minds, and hearts this week to receive the wisdom of our all-loving, all-knowing God.

SCRIPTURE

"The beginning of wisdom is this: Get wisdom, and whatever you get, get insight."
—Proverbs 4:7

Devotional

The idea of seeking the wisdom of God is often daunting to me.

Even Scripture itself speaks of the unsearchable depths of God. Romans 11:33 says, *"Oh, the depth of the riches and wisdom and knowledge of God! How unsearchable are his judgments and how inscrutable his ways!"*

But just a few days ago, we explored the untapped value of James 1:5 where Scripture says, *"If any of you lacks wisdom, let him ask God, who gives generously to all without reproach, and it will be given him."*

The tension of these verses leaves me wondering: how am I to access the depth of God's wisdom in my everyday life? How can I weave the knowledge of God into my own understanding so that even my normal life decisions—my thoughts, emotions, actions—are marked by the wisdom of God?

One of the most surprising revelations God is giving me this season is how available he is in my everyday life. While getting time away from the pace and systems of the world is critical every morning to attuning our ear to his voice, and connecting our spirit to his Spirit, that connection is meant to carry us into the everyday moments of life.

God longs to show up in our life as it is. Only the few are called to a life of asceticism. The rest of us are called to work, to families, to food and fun and celebrations of life.

And seeking the wisdom of God is meant to be a part of our everyday life.

So often, Jesus taught based on what was around him. He used the rhythms and season of nature, of family, of government and politics to teach wisdom to his disciples. Paul used the rhythms and systems of Rome to work, travel, teach, and proclaim the one true God in ways that could only be done through the constant receiving of God's wisdom.

To better ask for and receive the wisdom of God in a way that will truly transform our lives for the better, we need to learn to do so not separate from our lives as they are, but in our lives as they are.

Which rhythms exist in life to provide an avenue to receiving the wisdom of God? How in the midst of busyness can we better weave God's wisdom into our thoughts, emotions, and actions?

Rhythm One: Wake up to the wisdom of God.

Beginning our day seeking and finding the wisdom of God as found in his Scriptures, in his presence, and in his voice is the key that unlocks our ability to see God's wisdom declared through and in the world around us.

We'll look at this idea more deeply tomorrow, but if I don't begin my day finding the wisdom of God, it's almost impossible to re-center my life for the rest of my day.

Rhythm Two: Bring purpose to moments of stillness.

With social media and entertainment offering us opportunities to fill up every moment, even the still ones with noise, we have to be more intentional with our choice of how we use the gift of still moments.

Moments of stillness are a chance to catch a breath from the day, attune our ear to the voice of God again, simply rest in him, and reconnect our being to the Spirit. They're an opportunity to listen for the wisdom of God, to stop and notice the world around us and hear what God might be saying.

Even thirty seconds of stillness spent drinking from the reservoir of God's wisdom can fill us with what we need for the rest of our day.

Rhythm Three: Learn from our days in the evening.

As our days come to a close, it's so tempting to squeeze in a few more moments of entertainment or a few more swipes through social media. But there is vast wisdom available to us if we will bring our day before God and give him a chance to speak.

Asking for encouragement for those moments that most glorified him, asking for correction for those times we went on our own, confessing and receiving forgiveness and God's unconditional love provide a time for God to be our teacher and redeemer.

Rather than rushing from one day to the next, living with the same problems and questions, we can learn from our days with God. We can grow, develop, heal, and become who we know God made us to be.

The best way to do that is to bring our days to God every evening, adopting the rhythm of examining ourselves with the Spirit, allowing God's wisdom and kindness to transform us and refresh us before we begin another day.

As we move to a time of meditation and conversation, take the opportunity before you today to attune your ear to the wise words of God and allow him to offer you the wisdom you need to get the most out of your day today.

 MEDITATION

Take a moment to reimagine your life with these rhythms of wisdom as a natural normal for you.

Picture work, home, and time with friends with wisdom woven in.

Sit with that picture for a bit until you're ready to explore it with God.

 CONVERSATION

Begin by grabbing your journal (if you can) and processing these rhythms of wisdom with God:

1. What would it look like to begin your day with wisdom? Is that the rhythm of First15? Or is there some other tool or process

that would be most helpful in this next season for you? Invite the Spirit to give you wisdom and write down your thoughts.

2.   What do you normally do in moments of stillness now? It's so tempting to pick up your phone, get something done, or distract yourself. But what would you like to do in your moments of stillness? Process what it could look like with God.

3.   What do you normally do before falling asleep? And how could you repurpose a small portion of your night to glean wisdom on your day? How would that change the experience of your day?

The goal with rhythms isn't perfection, or even taking these recommendations explicitly. There are so many great resources and thoughts that can help you, but the choice is always yours.

Adopt a mentality of experimentation and see what works best for you. And if something isn't working, change it! This is your life to live with God, and perfection is impossible.

My growth tracker   S M T W T F S

ACTION

Choose to do one thing in a moment of stillness today, and one thing to do to glean wisdom on your day tonight.

Set a reminder so you won't forget, and experiment with these times to see if you can weave more intentionality and meaning into your day.

"Let me hear in the
morning of your
steadfast love."

PSALM 143:8

Wisdom of the Morning

DAY

4

In the Scriptures, we find the story of Solomon, a king blessed with wealth beyond measure because rather than asking for wealth or status, he simply asked for wisdom.

And as he gained wisdom from God, that wisdom brought life and abundance.

In week four of *Rhythms*, we're exploring how we can make room moment by moment to receive the wisdom from God we so desperately need. We all have questions that need answers. None of us knows the best way forward at any given moment.

Every morning presents us with a unique opportunity to seek and find the heart of God, weave our story with his story, and experience what true life looks like in relationship with him.

Today, may we discover and embrace the wisdom of the morning, to God's glory and our good.

SCRIPTURE

"Let me hear in the morning of your steadfast love, for in you I trust. Make me know the way I should go, for to you I lift up my soul." —Psalm 143:8

Devotional

Every morning begins with a declaration of God's wisdom. The sunrise declares God's faithfulness (Lam. 3:22–23). The song of the birds is voiced as an act of worship (Ps. 84:4). Our very awakening speaks to the possibilities only new mercies can bring (Lam. 3:22–23).

Every morning is an opportunity for the Spirit to open the eyes of our hearts to see and know that God is real, that God is good, and that God is present with us (Eph. 1:18).

But also, every morning without fail, I feel the pressures of life rush in. The pressure to begin work, to check social media, to sleep knowing the busyness of the day in front of me is at odds with the opportunity to seek and find the wisdom of the morning.

But my lived experience tells me that the more I give in to the pressures of the exterior life, the more I seem to suffer. As amazing as friendships, work, play, and action are, if that is all my life is, I become depleted.

This morning, as I made space to receive the wisdom of God, I sensed him offering a twofold approach to living an abundant life. Each facet requires each other, but we must begin with one before the other.

The first facet is cultivating and keeping a rich interior life. The second is developing a vibrant exterior life. And it's only when the two work together that we find the abundant life God so desperately desires for us (John 10:10).

But we have to acknowledge that the world we live in really only values our vibrant exterior life. It's what we do on the outside that is seen, praised, rewarded, even loved. We're expected to already be thriving on the inside before we interact with others, before we work, play, create, and interact.

Our lack of value of a rich interior life as a society, I fear, has led to the creation of hollow humans trying desperately to give what they don't have themselves.

How can we, in and of ourselves, have true and consistent love to give without receiving it from Love himself? How can we advance God's kingdom apart from the present working of his power? How can we voice the goodness of God when our own lives are devoid of joy, peace, grace, and thriving relationships?

In this series on wisdom, looking at how we can develop rhythms to take hold of the generous giving of God's wisdom, we must acknowledge the importance of beginning our day by cultivating a rich interior life.

Wisdom and a rich interior life go hand in hand. To thrive inwardly is to see ourselves as God does, to have his perspective on the world around us, to know and trust the leadership of our Good Shepherd, and to give over the ways of the world that we might take hold of the ways of the Spirit.

The one rhythm I want to submit to you today is: In the face of so many ways you can invest your morning, choose only to invest your first moments in the wisdom of the morning. Invest your first moments in cultivating a rich interior life. Don't live on the experiences of yesterday. Don't live from yesterday's connection with God's goodness. Reconnect every morning with the present goodness of God and learn to seek a vibrant exterior life from a rich interior life.

As we move to a time of meditation and conversation, may we seek and find the rich interior life God has for us right now. May we fellowship with his Spirit, take hold of his love, and be satiated in his love.

Take a moment to reflect on the different ways God is declaring his faithfulness and love for you in the morning.

Pick one aspect and sit with the goodness of it for a few moments.

CONVERSATION

Now grab a journal (if you can) and begin a time of conversation with the God of the morning:

1. Write down your experience of reflecting on one way God is declaring his faithfulness and wisdom to you in the morning. Unpack why it's meaningful to you.

2. What wisdom do you need from God this morning? Take some time and land on a specific question you can ask.

3. Invite God to bring you wisdom and pay attention to how he offers it in whatever form it might take. It could be a verse, it could be a picture, it could be an intuition. Whatever it is, seek to unpack all the meaning and purpose you can from it.

In my experience, there are usually layers of depth to the things God is speaking to us. Even getting a hint of wisdom from God can be life-changing, but allowing yourself the space and time to ruminate on God's wisdom can have a foundational, transformative effect.

Don't allow any feelings of shame or judgment over the time you have to sit with God, but instead celebrate whatever time you do have and choose to make the most of it.

My growth tracker   S M T W T F S

ACTION

Try to bring the wisdom you need to the forefront of your mind a few times today. See how it informs and changes even simple decisions, emotions, or perspectives you carry today.

"ALL HER PATHS ARE PEACE."

PROVERBS 3:18

Wisdom of the Moment

DAY

5

In the Scriptures, we find the story of Solomon, a king blessed with wealth beyond measure because rather than asking for wealth or status, he simply asked for wisdom.

And as he gained wisdom from God, that wisdom brought life and abundance.

In week four of *Rhythms*, we're exploring how we can make room moment by moment to receive the wisdom from God we so desperately need. We all have questions that need answers. None of us knows the best way forward at any given moment.

So often in life, we seek wisdom over large decisions or monumental problems but go our own way the rest of the time. But God has wisdom for us in every moment that, when received and implemented, has the power to bring even the ordinary to the standard of abundant life God has for all of us.

Today, may we discover and embrace the wisdom of the moment, to God's glory and our good.

SCRIPTURE

"Blessed is the one who finds wisdom . . . Her ways are ways of pleasantness, and all her paths are peace." —Proverbs 3:13, 17

Devotional

The foundational verse for our week's focus on wisdom comes from James 1:5:

> *If any of you lacks wisdom, let him ask God, who gives generously to all without reproach, and it will be given him.*

Most of us, I believe, will seek the wisdom and will of God when life gets especially challenging, or when we have a big decision in front of us. But I wonder how much of God's wisdom we leave un-accessed, how much of his direction and revelation we simply don't discover because we've taken the reins of our own life and are headed our own way.

In 1 Thessalonians 5:17, Scripture tells us to *"pray without ceasing."* I have honestly always wondered how it could be possible to pray always, to never stop the stream of communication between God and me.

But today, I wonder if there is a connection between these two principles, these two opportunities. Surely part of James saying that God gives his wisdom *"generously"* is related not just to the quality of his wisdom, but how often he gives it. But I also know that God never forces his good gifts on us. Even salvation is a gift that must be received.

So today, I'm wondering if there's a way that we can pray in every moment, to live in such a way that our lives are always open to the wisdom and direction of the Spirit, and in doing so, find wisdom not just for the big events of life, but for the ordinary moments.

What if, in every conversation, we were open to the voice and leading of the Spirit? What if, in every financial transaction, we carried both the heart of God for celebration of life and good stewardship? What if, with the decisions of how we spend our time, we carried God's value for connection to him, ourselves, and others and sought to both receive and give love in the fullest ways possible moment to moment?

What if every moment built on the last, reaping the reward of wisdom upon wisdom, adding eternal value to our lives and the lives of those closest to us?

The reality is, we need the wisdom of God. I need the wisdom of God. Left to my own devices, my life seems wrought with symptoms of my weakness. But when my moments are filled with the wisdom of God, I see God moving in strength and power in my weakness, somehow redeeming and working in and through me in ways better than I would have thought possible.

So today, as we move to a time of meditation and conversation, may we first recognize our need for the wisdom of God in every moment. Next, may we find that place of connection to the Spirit, that way of living whereby we can pray without ceasing from a place of true abiding. Then, may we find the wisdom God so generously is giving us in this moment, for the space and time we're in right now, trusting that as we take hold of his wisdom in every moment, those thoughts and decisions will carry us well into whatever the future may hold.

 MEDITATION

As we begin, take in the world around you for just a moment—everything, including the sights and sounds. Take some deep breaths, in and out, in and out, in and out.

Ask God to take you to the place of simplicity and connection with him in this moment. Lay every other thought, every other burden aside, and simply connect your heart to his, your spirit to the Holy Spirit.

Now, grab a journal if you can and take hold of the wisdom of the moment in conversation with your good and generous God:

1.   Confess to God if you are going your own way. Confess any sense of self-reliance or self-sufficiency. And receive the joy of God's forgiveness as he draws you closer to him in this moment.

2.   Ask God for his wisdom in this moment and pay attention to any thoughts, words, feelings, or pictures that come to mind. What do you hear him saying right now? What is he feeling? What does he want you to know?

3.   Now ask God for wisdom for something specific, even something small, and pay attention to any intuition you get, maybe a sense of peace or a sense of unrest. And move forward into action from a place of trust that God will lead and guide you as you do life with him connected, from a place of truly abiding.

The point of taking hold of the wisdom of the moment is not that you would stop making decisions or taking actions that simply seem good to you. God's connection is so much closer, his wisdom too readily available to ignore that he is working in and through your very senses and your life experiences. The point is simply to maintain openness to God, a posture of humility and desire for the ongoing leadership and direction of God.

As you practice the presence of God moment to moment, doing life with God should feel seamless and natural, not forced or debilitating. Every day, every moment is an opportunity to choose to live life with God rather than for God. And as you experience the fruit of a real, abiding relationship with your Creator, may he fill you with anointing and power to proclaim his reality and goodness not just with your words, but with your thoughts, emotions, and ordinary actions.

My growth tracker   S M T W T F S

ACTION

Today, ask God to give you one sense of revelation for someone else around you. Ask him for a way that you can be generous, give a kind word, or simply be present with someone who really needs a touch from God today through you.

Be bold and courageous as you seek to advance God's kingdom from a place of wisdom and love.

"In an abundance of
counselors there is safety."

PROVERBS 11:14

Wisdom of Others

6

In the Scriptures, we find the story of Solomon, a king blessed with wealth beyond measure because rather than asking for wealth or status, he simply asked for wisdom.

And as he gained wisdom from God, that wisdom brought life and abundance.

In week four of *Rhythms*, we're exploring how we can make room moment by moment to receive the wisdom from God we so desperately need. We all have questions that need answers. None of us knows the best way forward at any given moment.

Our world teaches us to stand on our own two feet, to have the capacity in and of ourselves to know which way to go. But if we will both humble ourselves and practice discernment, God has given wisdom to wise counselors all around us. We can grow and go factoring in the wisdom of others who have gone before us, or carry strengths and gifts we don't.

Today, may we discover the power of leaning on others and make space for God to bring us humility and discernment in his presence.

SCRIPTURE

"Where there is no guidance, a people falls, but in an abundance of counselors there is safety." —Proverbs 11:14

Devotional

Being fully transparent, I almost didn't write this devotional.

When I look at the landscape of Christian culture and why we lack wisdom, I feel that by far we leave too little room hearing for God directly while leaning perhaps too heavily on the words of Christian teachers and influencers.

But Scripture is abundantly clear that one of the ways to access the wisdom of God is through wise counselors. When I look back at my own life, I can see time after time ways that God used others to confirm or correct what I sensed him speaking to me directly.

For instance, there was this one conference that changed everything for me. At the time, I was in college and was struggling to know whether I should continue pursuing music or switch my major and therefore perceived career path over to biblical studies. I carried that question into the conference not really expecting to get a resolution. But after a service, a kindhearted woman I had never met came up to me and asked if she could share something she felt God had spoken to her for me.

She began to share that she sensed a spirit of David within me and that she got a picture of God on his throne, and me playing with his scepter at his feet, and how pleased God was with me.

While that may not sound meaningful here, it changed everything for me. As she shared it, the Spirit made his intention behind her words clear in the coming days. David was a musician, a songwriter, but that was only part of what he did. He was also a leader and a warrior. There was a time when music was his primary calling, but that time passed, as it was passing for me.

The day before attending the conference, I sensed God speaking the words of Jesus in Matthew 16:19 over me: *"I will give you the keys of the kingdom of heaven, and whatever you bind on earth shall be bound in heaven, and whatever you loose on earth shall be loosed in heaven."* I knew that whatever God had in store for me as I shifted paths would be to bind and loose things in heaven and on earth.

Proverbs 12:15 says, *"The way of a fool is right in his own eyes, but a wise man listens to advice."* And Proverbs 11:14 says, *"Where there is no guidance, a people falls, but in an abundance of counselors there is safety."* God longs to speak his heart, his will, and at times even his correction through the voice of loving counselors. Receiving and heeding the wise counsel of others is a gift from God, when given and received in alignment with the heart of God.

But understand today that not all advice given from others, even from those who are sincere, loving, and godly, is from God. Ultimately, we have to take everything to that place of connection with the Holy Spirit and seek what it is God would have us do. None of us are infallible.

In the story of Job, we see his well-intentioned friends offering "wisdom" that simply didn't align with what God was doing in Job's life. Peter and Paul, in many ways the fathers of our faith, didn't always see eye to eye.

The power within the principle of finding wisdom from others lies in holding in tension both humility and discernment. Every way in which God might be speaking deserves our attention. God does want to speak to us far more often than I believe we're listening. So we must begin with humility, taking in and considering the thoughts and advice of others.

But discernment is key. We have to measure the thoughts of others against our own and allow the Spirit to help us either take it as a gift from him, or cast it aside as we humbly and simply seek to do what is best.

Wisdom is best when it confirms what God is already speaking.

That means we need to already be seeking and finding the wisdom of God, paying attention to how he's directing us in all the other ways (scripture, our experiences, peace, the Spirit).

Lean into meditation and conversation around building a connection directly with God today that he might confirm what he's speaking through others.

MEDITATION

Reflect on a time God spoke to you through another. How did you know it was God?

Now reflect on a time when you needed to sift out something someone spoke to you. What did you lean on to discern what you were hearing?

Sit with the memories you have for a few moments.

CONVERSATION

Now, grab a journal if you can and take hold of the wisdom of the moment in conversation with your good and generous God:

1. Write down what framework you use to discern whether God is speaking to you through another. Take a few moments to assess it and invite God to refine or expand it.

2. What question do you have in your life currently that you'd like someone around you to speak into?

3. Pray and ask God to use others in your life as a sense of confirmation for the direction he's taking you.

The people God's placed around us can be a true gift, but we have to fight against the temptation to lean on others more than our own relationship with God.

God has placed you in the driver's seat of your life for a reason. His desire for you isn't perfection, but intention and faithfulness.

Step into the perspective of grace and enjoy the adventure of discerning and following the will of your wise God.

My growth tracker   S M T W T F S

ACTION

Ask a trusted advisor or friend for advice on a key question you have in your life. Take time to pray with them and discern what God may or may not be speaking to you through the wisdom of another.

"Keep them

within

your heart."

Hold On to Wisdom

DAY

7

In the Scriptures, we find the story of Solomon, a king blessed with wealth beyond measure because rather than asking for wealth or status, he simply asked for wisdom.

And as he gained wisdom from God, that wisdom brought life and abundance.

In week four of *Rhythms*, we're exploring how we can make room moment by moment to receive the wisdom from God we so desperately need. We all have questions that need answers. None of us knows the best way forward at any given moment.

Today, may we begin to create rhythms that help us to keep and use the wisdom God has given us through his word, the Holy Spirit, and our own life experiences.

SCRIPTURE

"My son, be attentive to my words; incline your ear to my sayings. Let them not escape from your sight; keep them within your heart." —Proverbs 4:20–21

Devotional

All week long, we've been focusing on both our need for God's wisdom and how we might seek and find it for God's glory and our good.

But the finding of God's wisdom means little if we don't learn how to keep it, or how to allow God's wisdom to build on itself until, from the inside out, we're transformed into a purer expression of who God made us to be in Christ.

When I look through the pages of my journal season after season, I am shocked at how often I need to hear the same thing, day after day, from God. What strikes me first is how loving and graceful my God is, that he would kindly share the same principles with me from his word, his world, and his Spirit. As a kind and loving Father, he is so patient with me.

But today, that has me wondering just how much better my life might look if I did a better job of truly holding on to the wisdom God has given me.

For example, what if I truly believed that I was fearfully and wonderfully made (Ps. 139:14)? What if I stopped questioning the ways God created me and his ability to redeem my past, leaned in fully into my wiring and my experiences, and simply sought to express myself as fully and lovingly as possible?

What if I truly believed that God had a pathway before every circumstance, and that I could receive and implement the wisdom of God at every turn (James 1:5)? And what if that drove me away from doing life on my own, leaning entirely on my understanding and lived experiences to make decisions moment to moment?

Proverbs 4:20–23 says:

> *My son, be attentive to my words; incline your ear to my sayings. Let them not escape from your sight; keep them within your heart. For they are life to those who find them, and healing to all their flesh. Keep your heart with all vigilance, for from it flow the springs of life.*

Perhaps the biggest opportunity within God's generous gift of wisdom is the ability to hold on to wisdom, to sit with it until it weaves its way into the fabric of our emotions, thoughts, and therefore actions and decisions.

You can keep wisdom from escaping from your sight. In God, you can "keep your heart with all vigilance." And the wisdom of God guards your heart and mind so you can experience the ever-flowing *"springs of life."*

So, with that desire at the forefront today, how do we hold on to wisdom? How do we keep it within our sight?

My first encouragement, or rhythm for you to consider today, is simply to sit with the wisdom of God a little longer than you might be used to. My own tendencies reflect the need for Paul's caution in 1 Corinthians 8: that knowledge apart from love can become an idol and lead to a reality of being *"puffed up."*

I love the experience of being filled with knowledge. But unless the knowledge of God finds its way to my heart, unless it springs forth genuine love and affection for God, for myself, and for others (Matthew 22:37–39), it's of no use to anyone, myself included.

We must make space for prolonged attention devoted to the wisdom and knowledge of God, to hold our hearts and heads open before God and his word, and allow ourselves to ruminate and reflect on a principle. We need to ask questions of wisdom like, What does this say about God? How would this have changed my past? What does this mean for my present? How should I act, feel, think in the future? And in doing so, make room for the Holy Spirit to illuminate and apply his wisdom directly to the areas of our life that need it most.

Even five minutes spent sitting in the presence of God, holding a wise principle at the forefront of our mind, can have an exponential impact in our lives.

But above all, afford yourself the same measure of grace your heavenly Father does as often as you can. The pathway forward, allowing ourselves to embody the wisdom of God, is not a straight line upward. It is a journey fraught with mistakes, propelled by small victories, and luckily saturated with the grace and love of God.

As we move to a time of meditation and conversation, may God empower us to take hold of his wisdom and to find ways to refuse to let it go, that it might achieve its full and beautiful effect in our lives.

 MEDITATION

Take a moment to assess the places you might be holding on to religion over relationship with God. Sit with those, with God's grace for a few moments.

Now, open your hands, take a few breaths in and out, and let go of things you've clung to that won't serve you any longer.

 CONVERSATION

Now, grab a journal if you can and take hold of the wisdom of the moment in conversation with your good and generous God:

1. Write down the things you tend to hold on to that are man-made more than God-made, even if they're religious sentiments. In what ways have they been helpful, but in what ways are they holding you back?

2. Now write down what it would look like to hold on only to the wisdom of God. How would that change the way you think, feel, react, and live your life?

3. What wisdom do you need to hold on to today? Get clarity and write down what of God's wisdom you need most.

One of the scarier aspects to an all-in relationship with God is choosing to cling to that which is best held in mystery. God is far too big for us to understand every facet of his truth. This world is constantly changing, as is our knowledge of it.

So much that we cling to must be held loosely, and few are the things that God would ask us to hold on to no matter what.

Find your security in the reality of relationship with God, more than the comfortability religion provides. That is the pathway to genuine truth.

My growth tracker   S M T W T F S

ACTION

Write down a piece of God's wisdom on something you won't forget about today. Keep it in front of you and allow it to guide you in and out of different circumstances.

Spending consistent time alone with God can be a struggle. We're busier—and more stressed—than ever. But still, we know it's important to spend unhindered time with our Creator. We know we need to read his word, pray, and worship him.

First15 bridges the gap between desire and reality, helping you establish the rhythm of meaningful, daily experiences in God's presence. First15 answers the critical questions:

WHY SHOULD I SPEND TIME ALONE WITH GOD?

HOW DO I SPEND TIME ALONE WITH GOD?

HOW DO I GET THE MOST OUT OF MY TIME ALONE WITH GOD?

HOW CAN I BECOME MORE CONSISTENT IN MY TIME ALONE WITH GOD?

And by answering these questions through daily devotionals, we help people practice the rhythm of meeting with God while experiencing the incredible gift of his loving presence.

To learn more about First15, download our app or visit our website: First15.org. The First15 devotional is also available via email and podcast.